THE CHANGING FACES OF

Botley

and North Hinksey

BOOK TWO

John Hanson and
Martin J. Harris

Robert Boyd
PUBLICATIONS

Published by
Robert Boyd Publications
260 Colwell Drive
Witney, Oxfordshire OX8 7LW

First published 1999

Copyright © John Hanson, Martin J. Harris and
Robert Boyd Publications

ISBN: 1 899536 40 X

TITLES IN THE *CHANGING FACES* SERIES

Banbury: Book One
The Bartons
Bicester: Book One *and* Book Two
Bladon with Church Hanborough and
   Long Hanborough
Botley and North Hinksey: Book One
   and Book Two
Chipping Norton: Book One
St Clements and East Oxford:
   Book One *and* Book Two
Cowley: Book One, Book Two *and*
   Book Three
Cowley Works: Book One
Cumnor and Farmoor with Appleton
   and Eaton
St Ebbes and St Thomas: Book One
   and Book Two
Eynsham: Book One *and* Book Two
Faringdon and District
Grimsbury
Headington: Book One *and* Book Two
Iffley
Jericho: Book One *and* Book Two
Kennington
Littlemore and Sandford

Marston: Book One *and* Book Two
North Oxford: Book One *and* Book Two
Oxford City Centre: Book One
South Oxford: Book One *and* Book Two
Summertown and Cutteslowe
West Oxford
Witney: Book One
Wolvercote with Wytham and Godstow
Woodstock: Book One *and* Book Two
Yarnton with Cassington and Begbroke

FORTHCOMING
Abingdon
Banbury: Book Two
Blackbird Leys
Charlbury
Cowley Works: Book Two
Easington
Florence Park
Grimsbury: Book Two
Littlemore and Sandford: Book Two
Oxford City Centre: Book Two
Rose Hill
Thame
Witney: Book Two

Printed and bound in Great Britain at The Alden Press, Oxford

Contents

Acknowledgements   4

Amendments to Book One   5

Introduction   6

Foreword   7

Section 1 North Hinksey Village   9

Section 2 Harcourt Hill   18

Section 3 Southern By Pass and Westminster Way   28

Section 4 North Hinksey Lane   35

Section 5 Old Botley and West Way   40

Section 6 Elms Rise Estate and Other Roads   48

Section 7 Eynsham Road and Dean Court   55

Section 8 Schools   66

Section 9 The Shops   78

Section 10 Medical Care   89

Section 11 Church Life   94

Section 12 Sport and Societies   103

Section 13 Remembering the Wars   112

Section 14 People   120

Front cover photograph

Ladies from Botley's Women's Institute in about 1930.

Back cover photograph

An Arthray Road street party in 1981 celebrating the marriage of Prince Charles to Lady Diana Spencer.

Acknowledgements

We would like to thank the following people who have so kindly lent photographs to us and revealed much information about Botley and North Hinksey: Chris Andrews (Oxford Picture Library), Mary Backhouse, Margaret Ballard, Geoff Barnett, Peggy Bates, Margaret Berry, professional photographer Frank Blackwell, Samuel Booth, Steven Braggs, Rowena Bunney, Cilla Brett, Greta Browning, Tony and Pam Carey (thanks for the photos sent all the way from Australia!), Jane Chapman, Jim and Joan Chatting, Mary and Brian Coates, Dr John Cockshoot, Dave Curtin, Brian and Josephine Dallimore, Jack and Clementine Day, Dick Deane, Dan Duhig and the Duhig family, Gwen Edgington, John Edgington, Amy Field, Bill Grant, the Guildhall, London, Francis, E Margaret and Diane Harris, Alice 'Maud' Harvey, Bernard and Jose Herbert, Robert Hicks, Jenny Holloway, Audrey and Clive Holmes, Pamela Holmes, John and Richard Jeffery, Jeremy's (Oxford Stamp Centre), John and Jill Kemp, Tom Kingerlee, Ted and Ann Lainchbury, Mary Lane, Pauline Lloyd, Matthew Arnold School with the help of Jan and Mike Deakin, Maurice and Mary McAvoy, the Warden and Fellows of Merton College, Oxford, Gordon and Rosalind Mortimer, Oxfordshire County Council Photographic Archive (denoted OCC Photo Archive), Stan Parker, Ted and Kay Parsons, Katherine and Kuppuraj Raju, Bob and Jean Rivers, Mick and Dawn Rivers, John and Beryl Rowe, Gerald Shirley, Thomas Photos, Oxford, Muriel Truslove, Janet and Michael Walker, Westminster College and Martin Astell, archivist, Evelyn Wissett, Janet Wright of 'Jaysons.'

John Chipperfield and the Oxford Mail (Newsquest [Oxfordshire] Ltd) deserve a special mention for their permission to use photographs from their archives and the help they have given us.

May we also thank those who have helped with details and encouragement: Dolly Ashby, Sarah Barker, Rev Rosie Bates, Julia Bishop, Pat Bishop, Vic Bishop, Blackwells, Botley Library, Bob Boyd, Chris Brice, John Briggs, Garnett Brown, Josey Carpenter, Gloria and Antoine Chavagnon, Vi Collins, Ann Day, Ted Enoch, Hedley Feast, Ian Gaisford, Marion Hainge, Alan and Malvina Harvey, Grace and Barbara Hawtin, Rosalind Hayward, the Isis Group, Maurice Johnson, Hazel Lepper, Pauline McKniffe and other former staff of Cumnor Rise Hospital, Briony Newport, Joyce Nickolls, North Hinksey Parish Council, John Read, Pam Robinson, Ernie and Nina Smallridge, Dorothy Squires, Mary Stewart, Gerry Thomas, Gary Walker, Beryl and Ken Walton, Sue and Chris Webb, Eddie Wheeler, Bret, Karen, Jim and Pat Wiles, Geoff and Mary Worth, Christine Zwart (editor of *The Door*).

A great deal of thanks is owed to Mike Berrie of the Ridgeway Military and Aviation Research Group, for the name of the pilot that crashed at the top of Yarnells Road in 1940, and providing much information on this tragic event A big thank you to any others whose names have been inadvertently omitted and we apologise for any unintentional errors and misleading information that are subsequently discovered.

Amendments to Book One

Since the publication of the *Changing Faces of Botley and North Hinksey Book 1,* many people have kindly come forward with further information and corrections. Some of this information is detailed below. Page numbers refer to those in Book 1.

Page 4   An acknowledgement should have been made to Rev David Rowland.

Page 14   Andrew Coles has pointed out that the landlord of 'The George' between 1987 and 1994 was Robert Charles Skelcher, commonly known as 'Bob'. In 1994 he moved to 'The Prince of Wales' in Jericho, Oxford.

Page 21   The motorcyclist to be seen in the lower photograph is Alfred Read, who was 'the only person with a motorbike in the early 1920s'.

North Lodge was built by John Parker junior, an ancestor of Stan Parker of North Hinksey Lane.

Page 23   The house to the immediate left of the Black Horse (bottom picture) was 'Broad Clyst.'

Page 28   A carrier called Max Mitchell, who was said to have been a great character, once lived in the house in the bottom picture.

Page 29   The Wheeler family, with their many children, lived in the cottage shown to the left of the blacksmith's and Seacourt Farm.

Page 35   Mrs Peggy Bates has corrected the caption to the photograph, which should have read: 'William Read was born in Botley in 1837 and married Emma Barnes. They lived in the cottage at the top corner of Hinksey Lane. They had seven children, including son Joseph who married Rachel Hedges and worked for some years delivering bread for the nearby bakery'. (The directory for 1932 showed Joseph living at Victoria Cottage, on the north side of the road.)

Page 40   The caption should read, for the second name: Bryan Jones.

Page 61   Second row, third from left is Audrey Shorter.

Page 77   The date on the first line should read '18th century'.

Page 80   The actual work on Ruskin's project began in 1874.

A note regarding the quality of the photographs.
Please note that the quality of the photographs included in this book will vary but where the photograph is of a poor standard it has been included for historical reasons or to make a valid point. We hope that this will not effect the enjoyment of the book.

Introduction

Whether you regard Botley as the gateway to the dreaming spires of Oxford or simply as a dormitory to the city, it is there and it has a long, interesting history.

North Hinksey too has a long history and the village, lying on the edge of both suburbia and river meadows, retains some of its rural character. It is within earshot of the A34 which plunges noisily northward into Botley, although now with a 50 mph speed restriction.

This book, like its predecessor, is concerned primarily with the changes which affected Botley and North Hinksey in the twentieth century. Change is not, of course, a twentieth century phenomenon. Matthew Arnold complained in *Thyrsis* that 'in the two Hinkseys nothing keeps the same', and Botley had already been bisected by several turnpike schemes. But within living memory this area has been subject to residential development on a scale barely exceeded in any other part of the country as Oxford reached across its flood plain to plant suburbia in what, until local government reorganisation in 1974, was the old county of Berkshire. Here is history, and people to describe it.

John Hanson

(Jeremy's Postcards)

Foreword

Botley and North Hinksey mean a great deal to me. Born in 1967, I have lived here for practically most of my life (from 1985 until 1988 I was at Wadham College, Oxford where there was a medical student called Evan Harris who later moved to North Hinksey and was elected our MP in 1997). I remember singing the teapot song at the Elms Road Nursery. Then I went to Botley County Primary School (returning in 1996 as a governor) followed by Matthew Arnold School where I performed in many a school play or musical; playing Malvolio in Shakespeare's 'Twelfth Night' was my favourite.

Then there have been the shops. I am too young to remember life before the Square was built behind Elms Parade but even in my lifetime I have seen quite a few changes. Through a child's eyes, Lanka's and Martin's were the ideal places for treats such as sweets, ice lollies or comics like *Whizzer and Chips* or *Look-In.* I remember patiently waiting in the queue at Martin's watching the children in front of me say, "I'll have one of those," pointing to various sweets as the shop assistant counted the cost up to 10 pence. In Lanka's, Vi Collins kindly wrapped up a box of Weekend Assortment sweets that I was buying as a birthday present for my mother; I was afraid that she would see what was in the standard paper bag.

Greengrocers such as Durhams, Gerrards and Dentons have made way for estate agents like Bradford and Bingley/Adkin, Andrews, Chancellors and David Tompkins. In Durhams, hard-working John Durham would bring a large sack of potatoes and empty it into the display counter. In those days, the staff served you and gave you the running total of your purchases as they placed each brown bag of fruit or vegetables into your carrier bag.

At Dorothy's, where you could buy materials like cotton and wool, I remember, in 1975, being fitted out with a pair of black corduroys which I later wore on stage at Botley School to sing 'Sleep My Saviour Sleep' in a Spanish costume (see illustration).

Whether in the shops or on the roads around Botley and North Hinksey, there have always been people to talk to and what friends and acquaintances I have made over the years. My mother taught me the importance of speaking to people from an early age. There was a Mrs Florence Baker, well in her eighties, who lived in Westminster Way. My sister Diane and I would wave to her when passing by her house, now and then calling in to visit until her death in July 1974. When I recently saw Mrs Bonham in her garden in Montagu Road it reminded me how we used to often meet her and her husband around the area.

There has also been church life. My attendance at church has tended to fluctuate over the years, but thankfully we have been blessed with some very kind-hearted priests from the different denominations. Rev John Crisp was a one-off. His enthusiasm for church holidays and entertainment in the late 1970s and early 1980s brought out the best in many people.

What other parts of Botley and North Hinksey do I well recall? I learnt to swim at Westminster College. I delivered many a free newspaper along North Hinksey Lane and on Elms Rise Estate. I had a Saturday job at Hartford Motors and my first full time job was at Grant Thornton, the large firm of accountants.

I realise, however, that much has happened in this area before I was born. Although my parents did not move here until 1957, my father visited relations in North Hinksey from an early age and attended Botley School when it first opened in 1938. Also, in the 1881 census, my great-grandmother's brothers (Charles and Dennis Bateman) were two plough boys, aged 16 and 14 respectively, at Seacourt Farm for the Little family.

Talking to the many people about what Botley and North Hinksey used to be like made me realise how little I actually knew about this place. I have learnt more about how the housing was developed, what it was like during the Second World War and who have been some of the important characters over the years. Whenever I go into the cemetery or the churchyard, I am reminded of those people sadly no longer with us but who all played an important part in shaping Botley and North Hinksey's history. I am so grateful to all the people who have helped with this book. Unfortunately, there was not time to see everyone but please do keep showing me your old photos and telling me about your memories of this special place.

Martin J Harris

A view of West Way in the late 1930s showing the Seacourt Bridge Inn and the row of houses following on from the Carey family's shop.

North Hinksey Village

We have taken the opportunity several times in this book to look at our surroundings through the artist's eye. Our first example is a selection of five photographs of North Hinksey, taken by Chris Andrews, a professional photographer living in the village. He has built up a collection known as the Oxford Picture Library and his particular interest in local topography is reflected in his publications, which include *The Oxford Scene*, *The Cotswold Scene* and *The Chilterns Scene*.

An aerial view of North Hinksey village and the A34, looking south. The turn to Harcourt Hill is at the bottom right. The willow-banked stream hems the river meadows to the left.

St. Lawrence's parish church, North Hinksey. Until around 1728 it was a chapel-at- ease to Cumnor.

College Farm in North Hinksey. In medieval times the property, in the possession of Abingdon Abbey, was probably part of the Ferry lease. From about 1600 to 1740 the property, including the farmstead, 100 acres and three cottages, was owned by the Finmore family. In 1740 it was purchased by Brasenose College, Oxford, as an investment, the rents going to buy library books. At one period it was called 'Library Farm'.

The ceremony attending the re-opening of a parish footpath by the 'Fishes' public house.

The hearth in Arthur and Margaret Berry's old cottage.

The Fishes

Landlords during this century have included, amongst others, Alfred Clark (up to 1913), Henry Ovenell (1913–1915), Henry Harris, Arthur Morris, Herbert 'Captain' Morris, John Beasley, and the Kirks.

Henry Ovenell with his wife, Lavinia. They later moved to the Eynsham Road and his grandson Ronald lived at 161 Southern By Pass, 82 Cumnor Hill before moving to New Barn, Stanton Road (off Harcourt Hill) in the 1960s until his death in 1993.

Left to right: Tony Worth (then joint managing director of Morrells Brewery), Kathy Kirk, Colonel Bill Morrell (Chairmen of Morrells), Kathy's husband and the landlord Ron, David Stockton (Vice-Principal of Brasenose College) (Oxford Mail and Times). This photograph recorded the official re-opening of the pub in 1984 after renovation. Until 1984 the property was owned by Brasenose College. The Kirks were involved with the re-starting of the Fishes fête in 1985 which had been held before the Second World War.

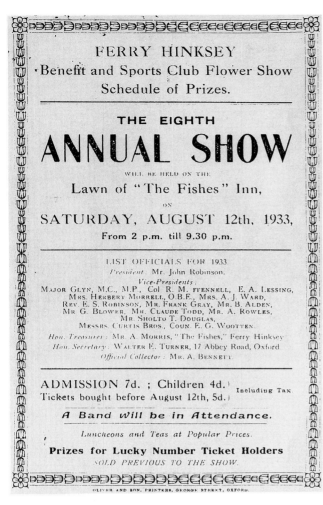

FERRY HINKSEY
Benefit and Sports Club Flower Show
Schedule of Prizes.

THE EIGHTH

ANNUAL SHOW

WILL BE HELD ON THE

Lawn of "The Fishes" Inn,

ON

SATURDAY, AUGUST 12th, 1933,

From 2 p.m. till 9.30 p.m.

LIST OFFICIALS FOR 1933.

President: Mr. John Robinson.

Vice-Presidents:

Major Glyn, M.C., M.P., Col R. M. ffennell, E. A. Lessing, Mrs. Herbert Morrell, O.B.E., Mrs. A. J. Ward, Rev. E. S. Robinson, Mr. Frank Gray, Mr. B. Alden, Mr G. Blower, Mr. Claude Todd, Mr. A. Rowles, Mr. Sholto T. Douglas, Messrs. Curtis Bros., Coun. E. G. Wootten.

Hon. Treasurer: Mr. A. Morris, "The Fishes," Ferry Hinksey

Hon. Secretary: Walter E. Turner, 17 Abbey Road, Oxford

Official Collector: Mr. A. Bennett.

ADMISSION 7d. ; Children 4d. Including Tax.
Tickets bought before August 12th, 5d.

A Band will be in Attendance.

Luncheons and Teas at Popular Prices.

Prizes for Lucky Number Ticket Holders

SOLD PREVIOUS TO THE SHOW.

OLIVER AND SON, PRINTERS, GEORGE STREET, OXFORD.

A Fishes fête programme from 1933.

Margaret Berry remembered how, in the 1920s and 1930s, it was mainly a produce show but there was also entertainment such as a man who danced on a spade! A greasy pole hung over the river and Beryl Walton (née Shorter) recalled the three-legged race, sack race, egg and spoon race and also bowling for a pig.

Ben Bird and Bill Orton in the garden of the Fishes in the 1930s. During the Second World War actor Geoffrey Tyrell was living in one of about 6 caravans in the gardens. He and other actors, who were working at the Oxford Playhouse, would often take children on trips to places like Bablockhythe.

The wedding of Mildred 'May' Hedges to fruiterer Frederick Mortimer of Cumnor Hill taken at Manor Farm where the Hedges lived. They married just across the road at St Lawrence's on 14 May 1914 with the service conducted by Rev Osborne Jones. One of the witnesses (probably the best man) was family friend Benjamin Bennett of 'Glenn Durran' in the parish of Cumnor (whose family had a laundry business). Frederick Mortimer started his greengrocer's shop in the Covered Market in Oxford in 1899 which was carried on by his son, Gordon, until his retirement.

May's sister, Violet Deane, and her son Reg in about 1918 with a view of College Farm behind.

A new house built by local builders Hooper and Jones sandwiched between the older cottages near the green in the late 1960s. The cottage on the right would soon make way for more modern houses.

The same firm built further house just accross the road in 1981.

When Jim and Joan Chatting first moved into the North Hinksey area in 1950, they lived in a Bluebird Challenger caravan on land owned by Miss Toynbee located between Ruskin Cottage (then called Rose Bank) and the next cottage heading south. They moved to Chestnut Road in 1954.

Margaret Berry (née Floyd) outside the house where she was born in 1916 with assistance from Mrs Hill, the midwife. It has been lived in by the family for just over 100 years since her grandfather Walter 'Pretty' Floyd first came to live there. In 1926 her father, Walter Floyd, was paying a rent of 3s a week. They purchased the house from Rose Launchbury in the 1930s.

Margaret's father, Walter 'Tricky' Floyd, taken at the rear of Ferry Cottage.

Gwen Edgington (née Howard) and her husband George in the mid-1930s. The cottages behind (Nos. 11 and 12) were at the extreme end of the village and opposite where the council houses were built in 1936. A more modern property now stands near the site of these cottages. Gwen lived in the non-thatched part as a child before moving to No. 10, which was the next cottage off the green (now replaced with a modern house). The 10 council houses were built by Messrs Harris Bros; the council agreed to pay them £3,240. Nearby was the 'Witches Elm' tree, which, it is said, got its name from the tale of Mark Scraggs/Scroggs who imprisoned 3 women in a hollow tree until the devil came to collect his soul.

The same couple with their children John and Jean in the early 1940s in the house opposite Margaret Berry's, which has been lived in by the Kilbey family for many years.

Harcourt Hill

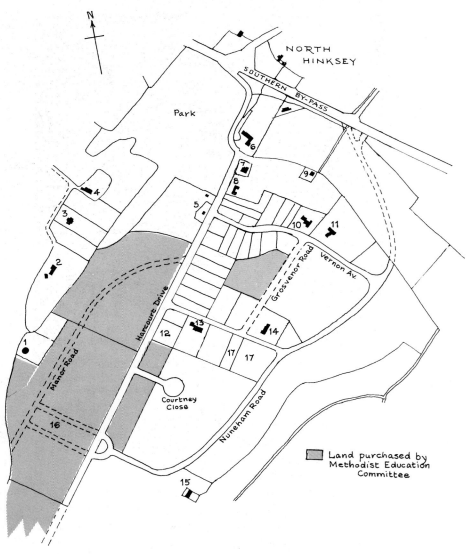

Map showing homes and features on Harcourt Hill in 1950.
Key: 1, Water Tower; 2, Sweetman's Close; 3, South Hayes; 4, Yarnells 5, Water Pumping Station; 6, 'The Fold'; 7, 'Hillside'; 8, 'Elmhurst'; 9, Well House (Conduit); 10, 'West Gate' (formerly Knowles); 11, 'Grayflete' (Sir Muirhead Bone); 12, Plot marked for Leadbitter; 13, 'Thatched Cottage' (Albert Betts, formerly Allchin); 14, 'New Barn' (Col. Isaac Sparrow, formerly Lancelot-Smith); 15, Old Barn; 16, Area envisaged in 1920 as village green for new community; 17, Plot marked for Vivian Jones (Halfacre House).

Sir Walter Alexander Raleigh, 'Knight of the Hangings'

Sir Walter Raleigh, painted by Francis Dodd (courtesy of the Warden and Fellows of Merton College, Oxford).

Sir Walter Raleigh (1861–1922) was Oxford University's Professor of English Literature from 1904 until his death. He had 'The Hangings' built in about 1909 (Hanging Close was an area of land shown on a 1740 map of the Hinksey parish), which was the first house to be built on an incline ('hanging' here means sloping) that later became Harcourt Hill, named after the Harcourt family who had owned much of the land in that area. Raleigh (no relation to his namesake of the 16th/17th century) wrote many literary books (one of his most well known publications was *The Planning of Shakespeare's England*), was greatly involved in the Oxford Pageant of 1907 and was historian of the Royal Air Force. He was knighted in 1911.

As a child, Gwen Edgington (née Howard) was given a goat by Raleigh which was put on North Hinksey village green to graze. On Sundays, when the children were going to church, if they saw Raleigh coming along on his bicycle, they would stand aside until he had passed. After waiting while he propped his cycle against the church wall the children would then follow him in. He opened Botley's first WI Hall in 1920. Raleigh Park was named after him. He was buried in North Hinksey churchyard.

Miss Winifred Toynbee, 'The Fold'

After Sir Walter Raleigh's widow moved out of The Hangings, the property was acquired by Miss Toynbee and re-named The Fold. Miss Toynbee was born in 1881 at 41 Portman Square, Marylebone, the daughter of solicitor Percy Toynbee. On her arrival from London, she was described as being 'dressed like a nun' and went on to be regarded as a hard working philanthropist. She joined North Hinksey Parish Council in 1934, the year it was formed, and retired from it in 1969 aged 88. She also served on Abingdon Rural District Council from 1954 to 1969. She had a chapel added to her house and on her death in 1976, aged 94, left her house to the British Council of Churches. On the land was a Jersey herd which provided many with milk. Indoors there was a parrot which would freely fly about in one room.

Miss Beryl Chambers was employed as a companion (as was common practice for well-to-do ladies earlier in the 20th century) and in later years drove Miss Toynbee about in a beige Morris 1100/1300. Previously Miss Toynbee had driven a Rover. Other employees included Charles and Gladys Seekings of East Cottage, Southern By Pass, and Reginald and Rose Gingell of Sycamore Road. Miss Toynbee was a strong supporter of the North Hinksey and Botley schools, as well as youth club facilities. In 1964, in recognition of her service to the community, a new group of houses was named Toynbee Close after a suggestion by Councillor Jim Chatting. After her death, Miss Toynbee's house was open to the public for viewing prior to the sale of The Fold and some of her possessions by auction. The Fold was sold to Barry Caisbrook.

Harcourt Hill was not given its name until 1938. It was to be called Harcourt Road, but Miss Toynbee felt that 'Hill' was a more appropriate title.

Miss Toynbee

The Wigg/Jeffery families at 'Hillside'

Suffolk-born Charles 'Hector' Wigg, headmaster of St Frideswide's School 1896–1932, having acquired land next to Walter Raleigh, had Hillside built and in 1910 moved from Broad Clyst (near The George in Old Botley and later lived in by John Curtis) with his wife Jessie and children. In 1924 Jessie's brother-in-law, Peter Tomkinson, had a bungalow called Elmhurst built on adjoining land. Wigg's surviving son Charles went on to be the vicar at Chearsley, Buckinghamshire, whilst his daughter Madge married John Jeffery in 1940. Briefly the newly weds lived in an adjoining caravan to Madge's parents, although they moved into Hillside permanently in 1947. From 1936 until 1942, the Wiggs lived in Chearsley and let Hillside to the Baker family. The Bakers' daughter, Elizabeth, married their lodger Dr Albert Sweet. The Sweets later lived in Elmhurst. Hector Wigg was on the parish council until 1948. Upon his retirement he was given an inscribed silver ashtray.

To avoid confusion with a similarly named house, Hillside was renamed Lothlorien (as the Jeffreys' son, Richard, was a Tolkien fan) in the 1950s.

Hillside/Lothlorien as it looked in the 1950s.

Sir Muirhead Bone (1876–1953)

Muirhead Bone and his wife Gertrude bought 'Grayflete' in the 1930s. He was a well-known artist, knighted in 1937, who was admired for his drawings of Oxford and his etchings. Sir Muirhead Bone was particularly noted for his drawings and watercolours of Oxford and he was commissioned to create illustrations by the University and Blackwells. At one time, local resident Gwen Edgington cooked and cleaned for them and her son John sometimes helped out in the garden.

Sir Muirhead Bone was married to the writer, Gertrude Dodd whose brother Francis (a friend of Muirhead's) achieved fame as a portrait etcher. They had two sons, Stephen, a successful painter and art critic, and Gavin, a fellow of Oxford's St John's College.

Blackwell's bookshop in Broad Street, Oxford in 1950. A colour painting of this now hangs in the shop with the main characters identified.

Many other notable people have lived on Harcourt Hill over the years. Sir Percy Meadon, who lived at Westgates, was a civil servant and chair of the parish council in the 1940s. Professor George Clark, who was the Professor of Economic History and fellow of All Souls College, was the first to live at New Barn. In the 1960s Sir Muirhead Bone's 'Grayflete' was lived in by Bernard Kenworthy-Browne followed by B J McIvor.

A winter view of Oxford by Sir Muirhead Bone from his home on Harcourt Hill c1950. The gasworks south of Oxford Station still marred the prospect and were said especially to annoy dons as their train drew into Oxford station. The gasworks were later moved to Cowley.

Westminster College

A Wesleyan Training College for Teachers was founded in 1851 at Horseferry Road in Westminster, London (Channel Four Television offices now occupy the site). After the Second World War there was an increased demand for teacher training places but Westminster College's plan for development were restricted by the Horseferry Road site.

On 12 May 1955 the Methodist Education Committee acquired 39 acres on Harcourt Hill from the Rt. Hon. Edward Viscount Harcourt and plans were drawn for a new college campus. It was fitting that the college should move to a site overlooking Oxford, where John Wesley had spent five of his most formative years as a commoner at Christ Church and where he was ordained by the Bishop of Oxford in 1725.

The first term started on 28th September 1959. The buildings were officially opened in May 1960 by the Hon. Sir David Eccles, Minister of Education.

A view of the new site in 1959. The design of the chapel spire, now a local landmark, was influenced by traditional American architecture. (Photo: Thomas Photos, Oxford)

The first principal here was the Rev. H. Trevor Hughes, who gave much care and energy to establishing his new community. Retaining its Methodist foundation, Westminster has been, under its principal Dr. Richard Ralph, a College of Higher Education, specialising in teacher education and the humanities, providing also a post-graduate P.G.C.E. and inservice training. In 1999 the college agreed to merge with Oxford Brookes University.

The Rev. H. Trevor Hughes 1959.

From the gardens of Westminster College a statue of Christ looks down on Oxford.

The Water Tower

On Monday 1 March 1993 the disused 120 foot high water tower was demolished. It had been built in the 1930s.

Workers who built the tower. Walter Floyd is second from the right. The house behind is believed to be South Hayes, at the top of Yarnells Hill, which was later lived in by Edmund and Primrose Warburg. A keen botanist, like her husband, Primrose was on the parish council for over 35 years.
She died in 1996 aged 75.

The tower just before its demolition.
(*Oxford Mail and Times*)

Raleigh Park

A view from the top of the park showing Elm trees, since felled due to Dutch Elm Disease, and a view of Oxford's dreaming spires.

Raymond ffennel acquired the Wytham Estate from Lord Abingdon and was an active member of the Oxford Preservation Trust. He was a German Jew by birth, named Schumacher, but made his fortune in South Africa. In 1930 ffennell, who was frequently finding his ideas frustrated by the City Council, expressed his thoughts in *'Oxford as it was, now is and never should be'*, a strange booklet composed in the style of Chinese tales. Concerning his gift of Raleigh Park he wrote:

'And it happened that lands belonging to the Great House of Har close to the City were to be sold. And a letter was written to the Chief Steward of the Great House of Har asking if the Illustrious House would sell for little silver thirty-three Akars of ground with many Old Trees as a Park for the people and children of Auks For. And the Great House was Gracious and consented to sell the land and the Old Trees for little silver.

And the Park was duly bought and offered to the Honorable City. And the man who offered it said, 'It is not needful to spend money on the Park. Is it not best made by Nature? And thus also will the cost to the City be but small, and the Park will in no wise be a burden . . . And the Park was graciously accepted by the Honourable Council; but it was soon forgotten, for was it not a quarter of an hour's walk from the Great Station?'

In 1993 concern was raised by Pam Johnston, chairman of North Hinksey Parish Council that Oxford City Council were intending to sell 90 square metres — a spinney near the top of Raleigh Park Road — to house developers. Valerie Wales of the Hinksey Fields' Protection Group and John Cockshoot, chairman of the Friends of North Hinksey and the Botley area of the Oxford Preservation Trust with the support of many others ensured that the sale did not go ahead and that a precedent was not set.

Southern By Pass and Westminster Way

In 1932, Miss Joyce Nickolls' aunt, Rhoda Rosetta Smith Nickolls, purchased land on the Southern By Pass and, based on her design, paid the building firm, Hinkins and Frewin, to construct a mock Tudor house. The following year, the aunt and her niece moved from near Walton Street, Oxford, into their new home naming it, 'Timbers'. It was the first house built on what was then called the Oxford Circular By Pass Road.

Other houses were soon built nearby including a house opposite, now in Westminster Way, which in the 1930s was called Highfield and was occupied by Joe Harvey, the bookmaker. This was closely followed by a house, since enlarged, which is now at the top of Yarnells Road on the northern side, which was first lived in by the Woodley family. Fred Woodley was a traveller for Grimbly Hughes and his wife Dolly (neé Field) was a dressmaker. Apart from a few houses, the surrounding area was mainly fields, some of which had the Howses' cows grazing on them. A Miss Greer also had horses on the land that was soon to become Stanley Close. Other houses that were soon built on the eastern side of the by pass included Mrs Curtis' house and the semi-detached mock Tudor property, also built by Hinkins and Frewin, known as 'Tudor House'. Mr and Mrs Taylor occupied the left part of this house.

When Timbers opened as a shop, originally it did not sell groceries but specialised in china from Japan, wool and toys. During wartime, when obtaining items to sell became difficult, the shop started to sell food and sweets.

In 1941, Rhoda Nickolls died aged only 57. Miss Nickolls was then assisted in the shop for many years by Miss Winifred Smith who had been a friend of Rhoda's. Timbers, as a house and a shop, was always quite busy with visitors of shoppers, friends and relations.

The shop was open from 9 a.m. to 5.30 p.m. during weekdays, although in later years was closed during lunchtime with a half day on Tuesday. Other relations would help out and stay at the house when either Miss Nickolls or Miss Smith was on holiday. On a Sunday, it was open from 9 a.m. to 11 a.m., which was very useful for the locals who had run out of groceries as well as those who came from the Botley Road to visit the shop. Some of the groceries were obtained from Oxford's Grimbly Hughes. Mr Woodley would take the order from Timbers to be delivered later. Children were thrilled to go into the shop and pick their favourite sweets from the jars or perhaps a sherbet dab from a box. So was Miss Nickolls. 'I loved it!' she recalled. Children would even bring visiting grandparents to see their favourite shop.

The shop closed in the late 1960s/early 1970s after Miss Smith died. By then the Southern By Pass traffic had greatly increased although residents of Stanley Close would still cross the road, albeit with difficulty.

Further down the bypass on the other side of Stanley Close was a house once owned by the Curtis family. Its location led to it being empty and falling into disrepair for quite a few years before being demolished to enlarge the adjoining industrial estate. Between this house and Stanley Close, the company Mobil had planned a petrol filling station, but permission was not given. (*Oxford Mail & Times*)

Since it was opened in 1932, the traffic on the Southern By Pass has gradually increased from practically nothing to over 63,000 vehicles in a day, which was counted by local residents in November 1995. From 1959 to 1961, when Stanley Close resident Francis Harris was having his house built on the other side of the Southern By Pass, he would easily cross the road with his wheelbarrow and equipment. Following the opening of the M40 extension link in 1991, traffic increased once more (official figures showed an increase from 41,800 vehicles/day in 1989 to 58,100 in 1994). After a public meeting in July 1995 called for by concerned residents, the Hinksey A34 Action Group was formed. Marion Hainge (later the chairman of the group) was a driving force behind the aims to reduce the volume, speed and noise of traffic on the A34. People from all sides of the political spectrum worked hard to get the speed limit reduced from 70 to 50 mph. In March 1997, Transport Minister, John Watts, unveiled the 50 mph signs.

Mary Stewart, who has been the longest resident of Westminster Way, came to her house when it was first built in the 1930s. The house was named 'Forsythia' after her husband's middle name 'Forsythe.' Her late husband Ken worked at the Oxford University Press. Initially most of the houses on this road were given names. Other examples include (comparing 1939 and 1949 directories):

No.	Name of house — occupier
30	Westover — Walker, Misses
32	St Brelades — Amond, Frank later called Blenheim Lodge — Whitlocks, ex-landlords of Royal Blenheim, St Ebbes
40	Michaelton — King, Albert
42	Rewley — Goodenough, Joseph
46	Kenville — Saxton, Lawrence — father of Terry Saxton
50	Egerton — Dix, Albert

No.	Name of house — occupier
52	Ranley — Warren, Sydney. Mrs Warren died tragically.
54	Helmier — Gibbs, Mr was Co-op manager in East Oxford.
58	Elmstead — Lockwood, Mr was Baptist church organist.
62	Audreyvilla — Parkins, named after their granddaughter Audrey.
72	Daubeney — Darvell, Frederick
80	Rovers — Taylor Mrs E

A picture of the by pass in 1964 during work to extend the dual carriageway further south from Montagu Road, provide the first pedestrian subway and extend the service road that was re-named Westminster Way in 1966. Just above the Mini is the Roman Catholic vicarage (located at the bottom of Yarnells Hill) which was demolished in the late 1970s/early 1980s. (*Oxford Mail & Times*)

The Isis Housing Association Self-Help Building Group

In 1952, Maurice McAvoy and his wife Mary, then living in a small flat in 23 Museum Road, Oxford, thought it would be a good idea to start a self-help group to have their own house built. At that time there was a shortage of houses and council house waiting lists could be quite long. Following publicity given about this project by the Roman Catholic churches around the city, the McAvoys were soon joined by a group of just under 20 like-minded people. The group was formed into a limited company with Maurice McAvoy the secretary, Ted Renshaw the treasurer and district councillor Dr Dempsey agreed to act as an independent chairman. Various sites in the Oxford area were considered including Hurst Rise Road, Eynsham Road (Noble's Farm), Dean Court, Norreys Road (Cumnor) and the top of Yarnells Hill. In 1953, Dr Dempsey, who was of tremendous help to the group, informed them of an area of land between the bottom of Yarnells Hill and Raleigh Park Road which overlooked the Southern By Pass, which the group eventually bought. Part of the land obtained was originally very marshy (referred to by some local residents as 'elephant grass' because of the tall reeds).This adjoined allotments at the south-easterly end. Almost two years were spent draining the land. The group members, who all had day jobs (some were in the building trade), spent at least 20 hours a week of their evenings/weekends working on the land. John Rowe was the clerk of works. Building started in 1955/56 and was finished in 1959. The Abingdon Rural District Council lent money to assist the scheme. Decisions made by the group were very democratic in matters such as the design of these 14 pairs of large semi-detached houses. Two spare plots of land on the site were advertised in *The Oxford Times* in September 1958 which were subsequently acquired by Francis Harris and George Haynes for private houses.

Foundations of nos. 156-8 overlooking the odd-numbered Southern By Pass houses. The detached house was built by the Brown family who had at one time lived in the house on West Way that adjoined the Careys' shop. (Frank Blackwell)

Note the caravan lived in by a family whilst the houses were being built and the detached house opposite (with two chimneys) which was the site of the plane crash at the top of Yarnells Road in 1940. (Frank Blackwell)

Construction of the houses showing the earlier 1930s mock Tudor houses. (Frank Blackwell)

A view from the site showing a track leading from the mock Tudor houses' service road. Although in 1961 a subway was recommended at the bottom of Yarnells Hill, it was actually built at this end of the road with the second one built in the 1980s by Montagu Road.

Members of the Isis Group. Standing, left to right: Matty Mulvany, Bernard Turner*, John Hanson**, Hugh Leyland, Don Taylor*, John Rowe. Sitting: Maurice McAvoy, Desmond Adderley, Ron Warburton, Jack Hemmins, Ron Faulkner, Ted Renshaw.
*Left before the houses were completed. **A different person from the co-author.

Other people who had been members during the period 1952–53 included Messrs Acaster, Baker, Baughan/Bourne, Collett, Howard, Kilkenny, Linfoot, Mullagh, Paddon, Roberts, Saltcastle and Tysall. Later members of the group were Perce Bartlett, George Elstob, Wally Lee and David Miller. (Frank Blackwell)

A 1999 re-union. Back row, left to right: Adrian Faulkner. David Miller, Maurice McAvoy, John Hanson, Ted Renshaw, Ron Warburton, John and Beryl Rowe, Hugh and Kath Leyland, Desmond and Nick Adderley. Front row: Thelma Bartlett, Kathleen Faulkner, Mary McAvoy, Sue Smith (née Elstob), Marion Miller, Joan Warburton, Molly Mulvany, Monica White (née Mulvany).

Above is an advert, from the 1930s, for semi-detached houses around Westminster Way (when it was the Southern By Pass)/Montagu Road. Some of these houses are shown in the photo below (OCC Photo Archive). The houses were built by Messrs Bayliss Bros./- Stanley & Co from Coventry. Further down the road where the Baptist Church car park is, there used to be a field where rhubarb was grown. During World War II, Emily Parkins, at No. 62, would see, from her front bedroom window, the military funerals in the cemetery.

North Hinksey Lane

This road was known as Ferry Hinksey Lane until its name change was agreed by councillors in 1938 to avoid confusion with Ferry Hinksey Road off the Botley Road.

Old Botley Post Office early in the 20th century when it was run by market gardener William Hemmings. The building was still standing at the outbreak of World War II. (Jeremy's Postcards)

Near the same site in 1964. Seacourt Farm is in the distance.

The Old Manor House

The following pictures show the Old Manor House before it was lived in by the Halliday family. The Hallidays used to have an antiques shop in High Street, Oxford.

The side view as it looked in the 1920s when the building was 3 farm labourers cottages owned by Stephen Curtis. The man outside could possibly be Ernest Hudson who lived there then (his cottage was called Davis cottage named after an early 19th century farm tenant).

A view from the other side showing part of the rear of the house before Shalto Douglas had it transformed by building firm Knowles & Son (Oxford) Ltd. Shalto later acquired Elsfield Manor, near Marston which he also renovated.

Looking from North Hinksey Lane after renovation (compare with the top photograph on the opposite page).

The renovated rear in all its splendour.

The stylishly decorated interior.

Willow Walk

A sketch of the 'Roman' bridge by Basil Field, a Magdalen College School teacher from West Way. Some locals recall how a toll used to be levied once a year when crossing the bridge.

A view from the same bridge looking towards the site of North Hinksey School.

The footbridge from North Hinksey Lane was often in disrepair until replaced in the 1980s.

The same bridge can be seen on the far left of this photograph taken between the wars. The foreground shows what a popular swimming resort it used to be. Some locals always referred to it as 'The Pool.'

However, sometimes the pool was dangerous. On 21 March 1885, five-year-old Elizabeth Ann Edwards fell off the footbridge in Willow Walk into the stream that was running swiftly. Amelia Castle, a 30-year-old mother, jumped in and although unable to swim, succeeded in getting hold of the child and carrying her through water of depths up to 10 feet to the river bank, no doubt helped by the buoyancy of her clothing. Amelia's sister, Fanny Harris (who married Francis Hutson at North Hinksey in 1886 and whose descendents became Humphris, the Nissan car dealers), was witness to the event. The

Rev W F Cornish, vicar of North Hinksey, wrote to the Royal Humane Society who sent him a bronze medal to be awarded to the brave rescuer. Amelia, who had recently moved from Ducklington, is believed to have lived briefly at the house now known as Ruskin Cottage in North Hinksey Village before moving to Cumnor.

Left: A pre-1919 photograph of Amelia Castle with her husband Thomas. The medal is attached to the top of her skirt.

The medal awarded to Amelia Castle.

Old Botley and West Way

A field belonging to Seacourt Farm, part of which was taken in 1938 for the site of Botley School.

The field in which the horse is standing became the site of the Hartwell complex.

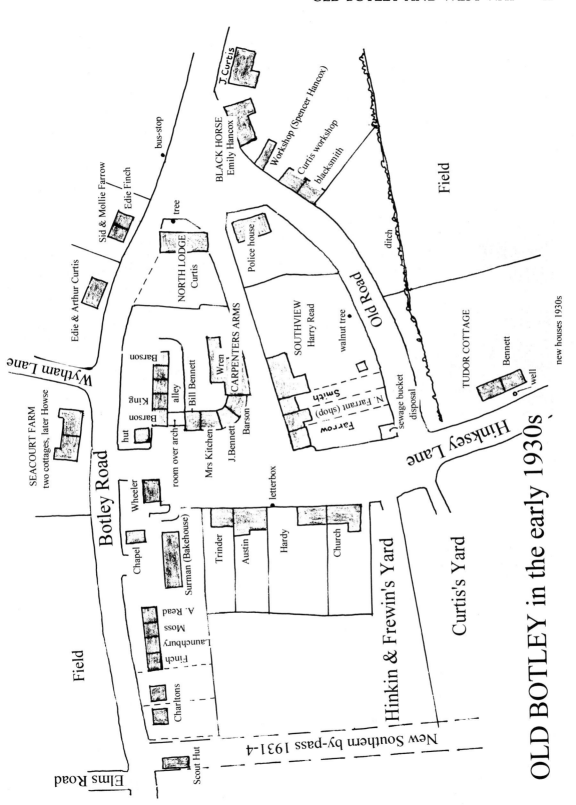

OLD BOTLEY in the early 1930s

Sir John Millais and 'The Woodman's Daughter'

A visit to Botley in 1850 by the young artist John Millais resulted in one of the most important English paintings of the nineteenth century.

Millais lodged in the cottage of Mrs King in Botley, probably the wife of Thomas King, a shoemaker. He later wrote of his 'Botleyonian privations'; indeed, the cottage meals were so poor (but no doubt typical of a poor working household of the day) that an Oxford friend rode out to Botley in her carriage to bring him a big meat pie. Millais spent a number of days in the woodland beyond Botley Lodge, in Wytham Woods, painting a woodland background. He was visited each day at his easel by Lord Abingdon, who made polite comment but on the last day complained that the background 'had not got Oxford in'!

The painting, 'The Woodman's Daughter', was intended to illustrate a poem entitled 'The Tale of Poor Maud', the story of a young untutored girl 'in the sweet age when Heaven's our side of the lark', befriended by a shy aristocratic boy. Of all the works by that school of artists, this was judged by many critics to be the most Pre-Raphaelite in character. (It was featured in the Inspector Morse fictional crime novel 'The Way Through the Woods' by Colin Dexter, and also the television adaption).

Millais returned to his London studio to paint the figures. The strawberries painted in the boy's hand were bought from Covent Garden for 2s 6d — in March. Millais wrote to another Oxford friend with a request: 'In the first cottage (at the lodge) there is a little girl called Esther; would you ask the mother to let you have a pair of her old walking boots? I require them sent to me as I wish to paint them in the wood. I do not care how old they are. Will you please supply the girl with money to purchase a new pair?'

The 1851 census records two seven-year-old girls called Esther in the area of Botley Lodge. Who was the 'Woodman's Daughter' — Esther Cummins, the child of a farm labourer, or Esther Carter, the daughter of a gamekeeper? Perhaps the latter, but either way, the painting aroused great interest and some critical controversy when it was exhibited at the 1851 Royal Academy Exhibition.

Portrait by William Holman Hunt of John (later Sir John) Everett Millais, 1853.

'The Woodman's Daughter' by Sir John E. Millais, 1851 (Guildhall Art Gallery, London).

The 'George'

The 'George' in 1991.

Commercial development at Botley now overlooks the 'George', which has provided refreshment for at least 250 years. In the 18th century, people came out from Oxford along Botley Causeway, in the evening, to drink, eat and dance.

West Way

The arterial A34, with its heavy, noisy traffic, crosses over West Way in Botley. The road rises up Cumnor Hill.

One of the Charltons' houses in 1959 just prior to demolition for the Botley flyover. Reginald Charlton's house was Willowdene (previously lived in by John Venables and William Plummer). His parents, Alfred and Ellen, owned Harmsworth, the house next door. In the 1980s, Alfred and Ellen had lived at 92 Southmoor Road, Oxford. At the time of his marriage to Maud Hedges of Manor Farm at North Hinksey church in 1916, Reginald was a motor salesman and his father was described as a grocer. Alfred was at one time the manager of Grimbly Hughes, a leading foodstore in Cornmarket Street, Oxford. The houses boasted such amenities as a billiard table and in the gardens were plum trees and a stream. An alternative to the flyover was a roundabout; both options were discussed by the council as long ago as 1955. In later years, Reg and Maud Charlton lived in Pinnocks Way. Maud died in 1962 aged 72 and Reg died 9 years later aged 82. (OCC Photo Archive)

The naming of West Way
The road from the old city boundary to Cumnor Hill was originally named Old Botley Road in 1939; previously, 'Old Botley' was considered a sufficient title. By 1945, the name was considered confusing with Botley Road and so, from suggestions of Cumnor Road and West Way, the latter name was agreed by the parish council.

The Seacourt Bridge Inn

The first landlords of the Seacourt Bridge Inn were Arthur and Gert Wiley, who had previously run the Osney Arms on the Botley Road for 17 years. On the Wednesday before the coronation of King George VI in 1937 they opened for business opposite what would, in a few months time, be Elms Parade shops. Following their deaths in 1950, the business was continued by their daughter Jose and her husband Bernard Herbert. Younger brother Mike also stayed on in the property for a while. Many a Botley character would pay a visit to the friendly pub. They included Blossom Trinder, Mrs Capel (who played the pub piano), Peter 'Giant' Coles, Eddie Wheeler, Harry(?) Pratley and the loveable rogue Bertie Coates. Mr Pratley would like to warm his beer with a poker and broke many a glass doing so. The Herberts retired in 1991.

The Seacourt Bridge Inn as it looked during the earlier years of the Herberts.

The beautiful inn sign which was removed when Banks took over from Halls Brewery.

Arthur and Gert Wiley.

Elms Rise Estate and Other Roads

Houses now rise up the hillside that was farm land until the late 1920s. Between the wars, North Hinksey parish experienced one of the fastest population growths in the country.

Arthray Road, shown above in 1981, was named after Arthur Raymond Howse, the son of the founder of Elms Parade, Stephen Howse. In 1938, discussions arose about calling a road on Elms Rise 'Ensworth Road' (Ensworth was a lease holder at Elms Farm in the mid-19th century). Objections were raised to replacing Arthray Road with this name and the newly named Crabtree Road was said to have 'geographical reasons' for its keeping its original and final title.

A view of Laburnum Road as it looked in the 1950s when it was just completed. Houses cost £2,000 with optional extras such as a kitchen hatch, downstairs toilet or own sideway adding to the final bill. Newlyweds Brian and Mary Coates moved into their house in 1956 having signed up for the house in May 1955 when the property was just a concrete base.

A steam roller putting some finishing touches to the road.

A picture of 'Elms Garth' in 1937. These particular houses were later renamed as part of Montagu Road. (OCC Photo Archive)

St Paul's Crescent in 1960. Some of the houses were built by Messrs R Gardner & Son with an original selling price of £695. On early maps a bowling green and tennis court were planned for the green. (*Oxford Mail and Times*)

St Paul's Crescent in 1999. One resident remembers: *'During the war it was like a jungle.'* In 1948, many residents were concerned about un-authorised dumping of rubbish and debris from partially demolished air raid shelters.

Houses in Chestnut Road when they were just completed by Minns in 1954.

The Fair Rosamund which was opened in the late 1950s. It was named after King Henry II's mistress whom he was said to have met at nearby Godstow in the 12th century. Plans by owners, Marston's Brewery, announced in 1998, to sell the site for house development were met with opposition from its regular customers.

A view of the lower end of Hurst Rise Road in the late 1930s. The semi-detached houses with the gable-end centre were built by Jack Coppock/Kingerlees. The original occupants of these houses in the early 1930s included the Day family at No. 11 ('Martindale'), the Worths at No. 13 ('Howsham') and the Blagroves at 'Windy Bank'(later No. 1 Springfield Road).

In the mid-1930s, a detached house was built in between the Coppock houses. A small part of the Cambrays' house, built in the mid 1930s can just be seen on the far right of the above picture . In the distance up on the hills are the Hazel Road houses, then called Southern Slope.

Miss Veronica Blagrove (back row, centre), who died in January 1999 aged 85, played Olivia in the Clarendon Press Dramatic Society's 1932 production of Shakespeare's 'Twelfth Night'. It was commented, 'Olivia's part demands a player who both looks supremely attractive and delivers her lines with the air of a young lady of quality, and both these functions were adequately fulfilled by Miss Veronica Blagrove.'

Louie Memorial Playing Field

In 1938 the parish council were trying to obtain land for recreational use. Landowners ffennell and Sholto Douglas had been approached, but H S Kingerlee of the Oxford building firm T H Kingerlee Ltd offered 14¾ acres of land south of Hurst Rise Road to provide a park and children's playground in memory of his second wife, Louie.

The Louie Memorial Playing Field.

The Kingerlee family. Top row, left to right: Jack, his wife Nora (probably taken before their marriage), and Carl. On the steps: H S Kingerlee and his wife Louie. The building firm's founder Thomas Henry Kingerlee (1843-1928) is buried in Botley cemetery.

A Yarnells Hill house exterior in February 1937, being one of the houses built by builders T E Knowles in 1935 that were to become Nos. 39, 41, 43 and 45. (OCC Photo Archive)

No. 41 was lived in by William Knight and was called Vyews; No. 45 was lived in by Kenneth Mitchell and was called Elm Gable.

The Yarnells Hill house interior. (OCC Photo Archive)

The name 'Yarnells' was the name of the area of land on which the houses in that road were built. A medieval holding in that area was called 'Arnolds' and so might have evolved into the name 'Yarnells.' During the period 1935–36, building firm Symm & Co. had at least four houses approved for building in this road. Others with building approved on this hill at that time included Hutchins & Sons and Mr Durham.

Eynsham Road and Dean Court

Tilbury Farm

Tilbury Farm, on the southern slope of Seacourt Hill, has been farmed for many centuries, though the present farmhouse probably dates from only the late 18th century. The origin of its name remains obscure. In 1943 the farmstead and its lands were sold as part of the wider Wytham Estate to Oxford University.

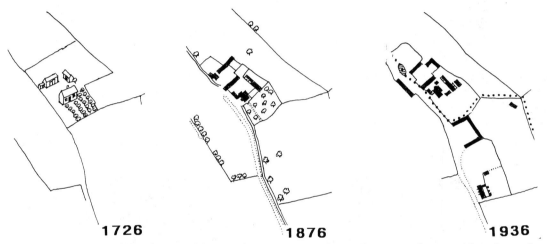

1726   **1876**   **1936**

A 1726 map gives only a pictorial representation of the farm, with its orchard on the south side. Almost every farm used to have a large orchard.

The Ordnance Survey (O.S.) map of 1876 gives a more accurate plan of the house and outbuildings, with the orchard still there. The farm had been mainly arable but the farming recession following the introduction of Free Trade made it less economic. Lord Abingdon reduced the rent and at the turn of the century it became a stud farm. It is said that one Derby winner was raised there. At one period the farm was rented by Halls and Baldwin, who were horse dealers. They provided horses for the cab drivers who served the Randolph Hotel in Oxford.

The 1936 map shows a large stable block to the south of the farm, while further down the lane Tilbury Cottages provided homes for three farm workers and their families.

Sketch of a steam tractor, possibly a Ransome, in use near Tilbury Farm early in the 20th century. It ploughed only one furrow and was criticised by old farmworkers because it didn't go straight.

Geoff Barnett of Tilbury Farm in about 1969, talking with the previous tenant, Arthur Lane, who farmed the land during and after the Second World War.

A view eastwards from above Tilbury towards Oxford, Shotover and the distant Chilterns. The land has been farmed for over a thousand years. The farm lies in a combe which marked the Saxon boundary between Cumnor and Seacourt.

Greys Close (No. 13) Third Acre Rise being built in 1937.

The houses in Third Acre Rise were built by the 'Botley gravel man,' Hubert Curtis. Ted and Kay Parsons were the first occupants of No. 13, which they named Greys Close after the piece of land it was built on. Near neighbours back then included Mr Whitcombe (Cleobury), the Howkins, the Oseys (their house, Tegdown, was later lived in by a Mrs Collins who had worked for them), the Kings (Mr King worked at the Bodleian Library) and the Hurrells. Ted Parsons (right) started work as a 'Bodley Boy' at Oxford's famous library and by the time of his retirement in 1980 was Secretary and Deputy Librarian. During the Second World War he collected many maps for his country. From 1964 until 1970 Ted was chairman of the Abingdon Rural District Council and was a former graduate of St Catherine's Society (later College), Oxford.

In 1999 (above), Third Acre Rise is a mature, leafy residential cul-de-sac.

The Wimpey houses were built in 1969 on and near the Eynsham Road. The three new roads were named; Deanfield Road, Broad Close and Owlington Close. Owlington was the name of an 18th century farm with the other two roads named after fields. Prices ranged from £4,950 for some of the semi-detached houses (without the roof windows) to £6,195 for the detached houses with a garage. (OCC Photo Archive)

Just further along the road (still in the section known as Botley Pound) in the 1930s appeared quite a number of houses of two different styles from land sold by local landowner Colonel ffennell. The house on the left (now a nursing home) was built by Walter Parker and his son Stan from North Hinksey Lane. A similar house at the Pinnocks Way end went up for sale around the time of the start of the Second World War. George Harris of Farmoor was almost tempted to buy, but in the end one of its first occupants was a bank manager. The other styles of houses were built (by Keep and Way?) on both sides of the road with wide frontage and bay windows.

A view of Dean Court from a garden in Cumnor Hill in 1944 before the council housing estate was built in the early 1950s to meet the urgent post-war need for family housing. A white cottage can just be seen in the distance on the left and some of the Third Acre Rise roofs appear above the trees on the right.

The Humphris family moved from wooden huts in Farmoor to a new council house in Pinnocks Way in the 1950s. Mother of the family Dolly Humphris (later Ashby), photographed here in 1999, enjoyed the great improvement in living conditions such as flush toilets and a bathroom. A wooden hut (donated by Boycott Franklin of Swinford Farm) later to become the Dean Court Social Club, from the very early days housed successful bingo entertainment organised by Dolly.

At one event in the early years there was a Miss Dean Court, Mary Gumley, with attendants who included Pam Humphris and Mrs Horne. Other members of Dolly's family on the Dean Court estate included her brother Bill Warner (with his wife Mary and family), her parents and her brother Fred in nearby Nobles Close. Joseph Howkins was the Dean Court Social Club's first chairman, supported by Pam Humphris (secretary) and Ken Howison (treasurer).

When the Pinnocks Way estate was built in the early 1950s, the planners did not anticipate that car ownership would be a significant factor.

Bricklayers Ted Keen and Eric White worked on these houses before moving into Nos. 34 and 61 Pinnocks Way, respectively.

Brian and Josephine Dallimore came to Pinnocks Way soon after it was built. Brian had been working for Boycott Franklin at Swinford Farm and they had lived with Josephine's parents in Farmoor. 'It was like moving to Oxford', Josephine recalls. 'There were street lamps!'

Some of the families who came to Pinnocks Way had been living in a squatter's camp at Tubney, a common experience in the harsh years after the war. 'It was a close-knit community then', residents say; 'you knew everyone else and people were always ready to help each other'. Most of the husbands worked at the Cowley factories and many worked extra hours in second jobs in order to keep their young families. Brian Dallimore worked at Pressed Steel, setting out at 6.45 a.m., and on many evenings went on to run a hot dog stand at Amersham. Stephen Leavy drove coaches to London and claims he didn't have a day off for years.

In the Dean Court Social Club soon after it was built to replace the wooden hut.

Looking west along the Eynsham Road from Dean Court about 100 years ago (Taunt, OCC Photo Archive)

The view in 1999. The brick house on the left was built by the Richards family at the end of the 19th century. They had the freehold of the land there and were poulterers and farmers. The house in the centre, recently built, is on the site of an old farm. Henry Godfrey left there at the age of 14 in 1676 to become an apprentice clockmaker and later had a shop in the Strand, London.

Dean Court Farm in 1970. William White then ran it largely as a dairy farm. James Nixey farmed there in the 1920s and 1930s. The building of the A429 Cumnor bypass bisected the farmlands on the slopes above and the landowners, the University, successfully applied for planning permission to build houses on the lower fields. The surviving farm lands were allocated to Tilbury Farm.

A rear view of the former farmhouse, a small part of which dates back to the 14th century, taken from what was once the 'Home Close'.

Looking across the fields north of the Eynsham Road in 1972, before the A420 Cumnor bypass was built. The present site of Fogwell Road lay beyond the hedgeline. (OCC Photo Archive)

A view of Eynsham Road houses in 1976 next to a large build up of soil that would become the bypass. (*Oxford Mail & Times*)

Just opposite these houses the Fogwell Road estate was built in the early to mid 1980s. Fogwell is presumably a corruption of the name 'Togwell' or 'Togles,' a medieval tenant who gave his name to land above the former farmhouse of Stimpsons. Some local residents recall how at one time the road was going to be called Fletcher's Chase. The houses in Orchard Road were built by Broseley and Costain in about 1983 with the others built by Thamesway and Macleans (with the dark window frames) in 1985.

Katherine Raju watching houses in Stimpson's Close being built with the rear of a Fogwell Road house just behind her. Katherine, along with husband Kuppuraj and son Alfred, would shortly move into their new house on the estate.

Fogwell Road.

Schools

North Hinksey School

A collection of school class photographs through the years:

A class of 1928. Back row, left to right: —, —, Margaret Floyd, Olive Wheeler, Kathleen Florrie, Doris Daniels. Middle row: —, —, Maisey Stevens, — Hudson, —, Betty Ayres. Front row: —, —, Freddie Floyd (head in bandage), — Wheeler, George(?) Butler, —.

1940 class. Back row, left to right: Jennifer Blay, Myrtle Pickford, —, —, —, Mary Ovenell. Second row: Michael Ovenell, Margaret Brown, Francis(?) Tilby, — Brown(?), Jeffery Blay, —, —, Paul Holcombe, Malcolm Frost, John Smith, — Bridgeman. Third row (seated): Jill O'Halloran, Jean Surman, —, Anne Jackson, Mary Stratton, Eunice Tilby, Betty Faulkner. Front row: Victor Bishop, John Floyd, Eddie Wheeler, Rodney Ellis, Arthur Surman.

1948 class. Back row, left to right: –, Pamela Huckings (later Cudmore), Janet Miles, Gill Broome (later Pratley), Dinah Castle, Pat Brock, Jean Orton (later Rivers). Middle row: –, Philip Russell, Stanley –, Bob Gillman, John Langham, John Freel, Eddie Bishop, –. Front row: Judith Clare, Doreen Weller, –, Michael Faulkner, Jeanette Brock, Gale Stroud, Diane Level.

Slow bicycle race in St Peter's College sportsground. John Day is the middle child.

In June 1976, North Hinksey School held a Tudor evening as part of Botley Community Festival. Due to the local connection of Walter Scott's novel 'Kenilworth' first published in 1821 (it featured the death of Amy Robsart at Cumnor Place, Cumnor), the school hall became Kenilworth Castle and Wolfson College's head chef, Tony Willis, provided Elizabethan style food. The children also re-enacted the 'Kenilworth' story. Included in the picture are Sarah Coppock and Julie Swadling. (*Oxford Mail & Times*)

The festival was held from 5 to 13 June with the aim of bringing the community together. Botley Baptist minister, Rev Philip Clements-Jewery, was the secretary of the festival committee. The timetable of events was:

Saturday 5th June	Drama from Westminster College Students
Weekend	Darts competition at Dean Court Social Club
	Historical exhibition at College Farm
	Bellringers at St Lawrence
Monday 7th June	Road Safety Quiz in Church Hall, West Way
Tuesday 8th June	Choral and orchestral concert in Church Hall
Wednesday 9th June	Judo demonstration at Botley Youth Centre
Thursday 10th June	Folk evening at Elms Court
Friday 11th June	Tudor evening at North Hinksey Primary School
Saturday 12th June	Festival dance at Elms Court
Sunday 13th June	Inter-pub tug-of-war by Seacourt Stream in North Hinksey Lane

Botley Pre-School

Botley Pre-School was founded in the mid-1970s, first meeting in St Peter & St Paul's Church Hall. They later transferred to the Baptist Hall before moving to their own building in April 1991 in Elms Road between the nursery and primary school. This was achieved through the hard work of local people and much earnest fundraising. Some of the key people involved in this success were Rona and David Sellick (who was then the community police officer), Kim and Dave O'Brien, Pete Fox, Roland Harris, Wendy Faulkner, Annabelle Dee, Janet and Jim Dobson.

Dave Sellick in the doorway and Roland Harris working on the desk, preparing the Elms Road building.

Wendy Faulkner leading the children (aged 2½ to 5) in a circle. Clockwise from Wendy: Robert Clanfield, Stephanie Brown, Jessica Fuzzey, George Lawty, Mark Rayson, Kezia Edridge, Manveer Kalsi, Hollie Roberts, Mitchell Roberts, Sophie Townsend, Georgia Wren, Megan Winch, Jack Ross, Joseph Owen.

Harmsworth Kindergarten School

Harmsworth Kindergarten School was accommodated in a building behind the 'tin church' which formerly stood near the present site of St Peter & St. Paul's. The principal in the 1940s was Mabel Clarke, who lived near Quaking Bridge in Oxford.

Robert Hicks, whose parents then lived in the Garth, off Montagu Road, remembers the school going for swimming lessons at a little loop in the Seacourt Stream near the 'George'. They also went for nature walks along the old Wytham road.

To get to school he climbed a stile off Arthray Road (where the car park entrance is now) which gave access to the orchard behind Elms Parade and the farm. Behind the Parade, near a second stile, was a hut used by Mr. Taylor, the watch repairer and Jeweller.

Robert Hicks later joined the family business: T A Hicks (formerly called Hicks & Son (Oxford) Ltd.), wholesale fruit merchants (the 'Covent Garden of Oxford'), which had moved in 1939 from Cowley to Ferry Hinksey. It supplied customers for 50 miles around.

Pupils at Harmsworth Kindergarten in 1947—8. In the top row: third from left Penelope Smythe; fourth Pamela Jefferies; far right Bobby Jefferies. Front row: first left Robert Hicks.

A kindergarten group 1948—9. Middle row: second from left Penelope Smythe. Sitting on ground, on left Robert Hicks.

The Harmsworth Kindergarten School.

REPORT FOR THE TERM ENDING *2nd April 1948*

Name *Robert Hicks.*

Times absent { Morning *4* / Afternoon *4*   Times Late { Morning *3* / Afternoon *4*

Arithmetic	*Excellent progress.*
Brush Work	
Chalking	*Much improved.*
Designing	*Pleasing progress*
Dictation	
English	
Geography	*Shows great interest.*
Handwork	*Much progress.*
History	*Shows great interest.*
Modelling	*Still poor.*
Nature Study	*Listens most attentively.*
Poetry	*Good.*
Reading	*Excellent progress. Delightful effort made.*
Scripture	*Likes this subject.*
Writing	*Pleasing progress*

General Remarks: *Has worked extremely well throughout the term.*

Conduct: *Very good*

Next Term begins *Wednesday 28th April*   Ends *Wednesday 28th July 1948.*

Mabel Clarke ____ Principal

Part of Robert Hicks' school report. Note the range of subjects covered.

The view in 1999 of Church Way, showing the entrance to the car park, where formerly a stile gave access to a footpath to the school through Elms Farm orchard. As late as the 1960s, mini-fairs were held on the site of this car park.

Elms Road Nursery School

A wartime nursery was established by Social Services in 1943 for children whose mothers were engaged in war work. It was one of the first in Berkshire. In 1948 it was taken over by Berkshire Education Department to become a Nursery School for 3–5 year olds under a teacher-trained Head. Until 1977 that Head was Miss Bull, known to her friends as 'Johnny'. She was assisted by qualified Nursery Nurses.

Miss 'Johnny' Bull on her retirement in July, 1977. 'Yes, I've enjoyed my 30 years with the school. It's been my life.'

Muriel Truslove, a teacher at the school for 15 years, recalls that it was always a very happy school, due to the good teamwork established by Miss Bull. Her skill and experience brought her invitations to demonstrate teaching of pre-school children in the United States. There were many learning activities, but also games and recreations such as music and play.

A day out. Children going on a visit to Didcot nursery school in 1975, accompanied by Muriel Truslove (light coat), county adviser Chris Jarman (left), and parents. Festivals such as Harvest, Mother's Day, Easter and Christmas provided chances for cooking (with help from Kathleen Wigger in the kitchen) and making decorations. Events such as the first Moon Landing aroused a special excitement and interest.

Rosalind Hayward brought her horse 'Henry' from Miss Pat Halliday's stables in North Hinksey Lane to meet the children in c.1970. Miss Hilton was to the left of her.

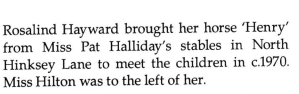

'I wish....' Freddy Elliot stirring the Christmas pudding in 1985. Mark was to the left behind him.

Harvest Festival 1992. Cakes were made to share with parents and staff. On the right, Faye Robinson, nursery nurse; on the left, Evelyn, special needs support staff, with Jason Manito on her knee. Gift boxes on the table were ready for distribution.

Muriel Truslove remembers that conditions were not easy in the early days. Not until 1970 were the coke stoves replaced with central heating. Over more than 50 years, hundreds of children have passed through the school, benefitting from learning in the company of each other and with the guidance of staff. Today, under Oxfordshire County Council, it continues to meet an important need.

Botley School

(For further details please see *The History of Botley School 1938–1998,* by Martin J Harris, Terry Peedell and Monica White.)

An aerial view of the school also showing the adjoining nursery. This picture shows the open quad which was enclosed with glass partitions in 1967.

A group of people standing just outside the school in the 1940s. Left to right: Mrs Waugh (teacher), Mrs Phipps (teacher), Mr Thomas (chairman of governors), Miss Caudwell (teacher), Mr Harber (headmaster 1938–1955), Miss Winifred Toynbee (governor), Mrs Knight (teacher), Mrs Florence Stevens (teacher). Mr Harber was also chairman of the parish council from 1949 until 1952.

Four headteachers covering the years from 1973 to the present day. Left to right: John Batey (1987–1993), Patricia Pritchard (1993–), Michael Cantrell (1973–1979), Martin Cox (1979–1986).

Some of the pupils who attended on the first day on 26 April 1938 were re-united on the school stage in 1998, the diamond jubilee year. Left to right: Patricia Pritchard (headteacher), Sylvia Rivers (née Theobald), – , John Read, Miss Ruth Woodward (teacher 1938–77), –, Nancy Wright (née Enoch), Harold Bishop, Cedric Tyrell, Charlie Syrett, Francis Harris, Michael Daniels, Stuart Munt, Ted Enoch.

Matthew Arnold School

Glyn Davies, after spending three years as head of Botley School, took his older pupils with him to become the first head of Matthew Arnold School when it opened on 9 September 1958. After training at Bangor from 1928 to 1930, Davies taught in Lancashire and at Anglesey before serving as a flying officer in the Royal Air Force during the Second World War. After a further period in Lancashire he joined the Royal Ascot Church of England School as senior master. He was promoted to headmaster in 1949 and remained there until his move to Botley. He retired in 1972 and died in the 1980s.

The school's first deputy head was former evacuated teacher Mrs Barbara Stewart and Mr G Platt was senior master. The school was designed by Berkshire County Architect, Mr J T Castle, and was built by local building firm Kingerlee Ltd at a cost of about £125,000. Liz Howarth, who replaced Joseph Newman as headteacher, retired at the end of 1998. Her successor was ex-BBC sound engineer, Adrian Percival who joined the school in April 1999.

Glyn Davies, sat between Vernon Howells and Jean Bickley, with the teachers of 1972–73.

The Shops

Ian Gaisford and Gary Walker cutting a customer's hair in the Elms Parade barbers. Ian's father Maurice started his own business on this site in the early 50s having trained at Cecil Smith's on the Botley Road (now a Post Office) and having worked at Stranges. At around the same time his wife and son moved from Donnington to a new house at 69 Hurst

Rise Road. Brother John Gaisford worked for the Oxford Mail and the other brothers Keith, Dennis and Haydn ('Mutch') also helped out with the hairdressing. After his apprenticeship, son Ian joined in the early '70s working alongside his dad and Jim Windle. Maurice Gaisford died in 1982. Ian and Gary for quite a few years have also sold local history books, including the 'Changing Faces' series.

Until her retirement in early 1999, Grace Hawtin ran her ladies' hairdresser's above Gaisford's. Over the road Janet Wright has been cutting and styling ladies' hair at Jaysons for well over 25 years. She took over from John Tompkins in the early 1970s. Her parents, Mr and Mrs Lawrence Pancott came to live at 28 Southern Slope (now Seacourt Road) in 1935.

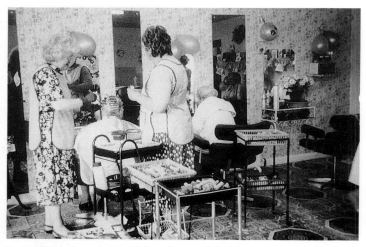

Janet Wright assisted by Jenny Manion with 2 of their customers in the mid 90s.

No 4 Elms Parade has been best remembered for the greengrocers Durhams. For many years John Durham, his family and a handful of loyal staff served the customers (before the self-service days came along), adding up the prices in their head as they went along. One of the earliest greengrocers in this shop was Henry Smart, a short man with a red face.

John Durham's daughter Sue peering through the shop window adorned with Hallowe'en pumpkins in 1976. Sue went on to open Sue's Flower Shop at no. 9 (formerly Palmer's wine shop and Shirley Smith of Oxford Ltd dyers & cleaners). (Oxford Mail & Times)

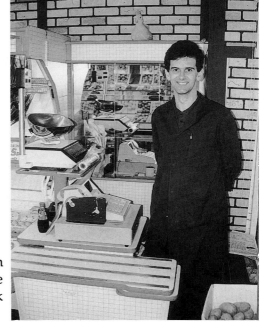

After the death of his wife Bett, John Durham handed over the reigns to Colin Luck before the shop was closed in April 1998. Colin Luck in the shop during its final week.

No. 5 Elms Parade has gradually developed from being a fishmonger's run by T Byard & Son in 1938 to being Jordan's pet food shop.

In the late 1940s, Sheffield born Sam Booth took over the shop and encouraged business by cycling around the area announcing his visits by ringing his bell. His interest in Botley developed as he acquired property and had a shop built since used by Jaysons, Parsons & Riley and the model shop.

Until his death in 1967, no. 6 Elms Parade was the chemist's shop run by John Wissett, who had come from the Botley Road chemist's having studied at the Liverpool School in Pharmacy. Along with his wife Evelyn and son David they initially lived in flat 6 above what was then 'Eve,' the newsagent, confectioner's and tobacconist's run by Miss Eve Jennings who lived at no. 7 Finmore Road.

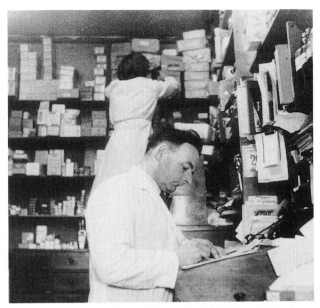

Mr Wissett with assistant Doreen Robbins (née Kirby) who also worked for Mr Wissett's successor Bernard Pottle.

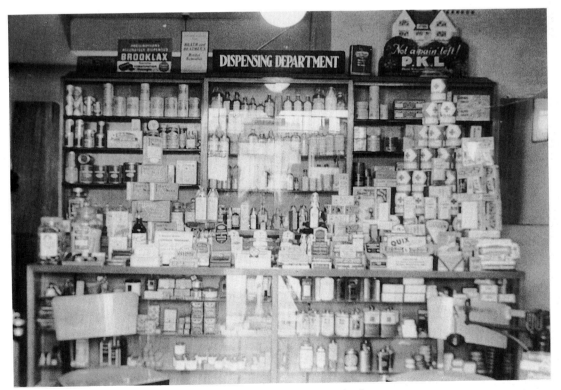

The interior of Mr Wissett's shop.

The middle 3 Elms Parade shops as they looked in 1956. (Oxford Mail & Times). Between Wissett's and Barclays Bank (with manager Tom Dwelly) was Ernest Shirley's ironmonger's shop.

The shop front in 1999, which is the only shop to retain the original window frame style. Gaisford's is the only one to still have its blue lettering above the shop

The Shirleys originally had their ironmongers' shop at no. 8 Elms Parade (later occupied by Courtney's, Barclays Bank, a bookmakers and Crown Prints) in the late 1930s before moving next door to no. 7 where they remained until the early 1960s assisted by Mrs Shirley's sister, Miss Edith Long. The family, who originated from Jericho, had been living in Cambridge, where Ernest, who had an astronomy degree from Oxford's St Catherine's Society (later College), was working as an astronomer. They moved to their new house, 15 Montagu Road which was then called 6 Elms Garth. From 1947-1964 they lived at 16 Yarnells Hill, which had been built by Eynsham builders, the Hill brothers, on land previously owned by the building firm Hinkins & Frewin. In 1956, Gerald joined solicitors Linnell & Murphy, where he remained until his retirement in the mid 1990s. From 1968 Gerald worked in the Botley branch for over 20 years.

Daughter Marion and Ernest Shirley. Friend Ivy Bossom, Frances Shirley. Taken in 1985 on the occasion of the Shirleys' golden wedding anniversary.

The Shirleys' children Gerald and Marion outside the back of their Montagu Road house in the 1940s.

Lanka and A Watson & Sons Ltd in 1959. (Oxford Mail & Times)

Watsons and Eve. Lanka and Watsons eventually swapped premises so that Lanka and Eve could become one shop. Mr Judt (often known as Mr Lanka) would serve many delighted children in his shop with assistance from staff such as Vi Collins and Mrs Giles. Mr Judt's wife Evelyn (1901-1995) was a member of the Howse family. (Oxford Mail & Times)

Courtney's bike shop (right) which although next to no. 12 was no. 14. In the 1970s it was a toy shop run by Bella Beechey (later Malvina Harvey and finally John Driscoll before it was changed to a motorist's shop).

Botley shopping centre (below), as it looked in 1969 before the 1980s re-vamp. (Oxford Mail & Times) Before Pottle's chemist shop (later taken over by Lloyd's) moved next to Martin's, it was home to a laundrette and a sauna bath. Bishops was originally located where the Apollo 2000 electrical store has been since the 1990s. Keith and Sandra Baughan, took over the jeweller's shop from Mr Taylor. By 1999, they had been in the shopping centre for 23 years.

Russian-born Coco the Clown (real name Nicolai Polakovs, 1900-1974), opened Bishops in Botley shopping precinct on 29 February 1968 with Deidre Pilgrim, Miss Lyons Tea. Coco, a star of Bertram Mill's Circus, handed out road safety badges to the delighted children. (Oxford Mail & Times)

In August 1975, Bishops moved to a new site next to the fish and chip shop. In 1983 the staff were honoured by Bishops headquarters for their good manners. Store manager, Charlie Haynes is seen here receiving the cup from Bishop's managing director Nigel Harvey in front of some of the staff. Left of Nigel: Maureen Collins (later Robinson), Nick Deacon, Mick Havard. Between Nigel and Charlie: Laurie –, Sue Tideswell, Sarah –, –, – (man hidden), Beryl Eagle. Right of Charlie: Maureen Towill, –, Vera Coombs. (Oxford Mail & Times). Maureen Collins appeared on the TV show 'The Golden Shot' in the 1970s when it was presented by Norman Vaughan. Pop star Gene Pitney was a guest on the programme.

The Careys' shop

Ernest George Carey, who had lived in Osney when young, came to Botley in the 1920s, having been the post master in Horspath village. He, his wife Lucy (née Woods) and their 4 children Cecil, Hilda (known as Dorothy), Frankie (killed in a road accident as a child), and Peggy lived above the family run grocer's and post office shop on the corner of Poplar Road and what is now West Way. Lucy died of TB, Ernest Carey later married Winifred May Giles in 1932, whose sister Mary with her husband George moved to one of the Tilbury Farm cottages in the 1930s. Winifred had 3 sons: Tony (1933-), Patrick (1935-1998) and Bob (1939-1960). The late Lucy's mother lived at the shop with the second family until she died aged 101. The Post Office part of the shop was down the right hand side. Many hours would be spent, after the shop closed, counting receipts from pension books and putting them in piles according to their colour and value. Ernest Carey was also a local parish councillor. In about 1943, Ernest and Winifred Carey retired, selling the shop to the Co-op and moving to no. 62 West Way on the corner of Elms Road. Ernest died in 1962, aged 74 shortly followed by Winifred in 1964, aged only 57.

Ernest Carey with son Patrick at the rear of the shop in about 1939.

Winifred Carey in 1963.

Tony Carey, in 1951, sat behind John Hancox, son of the former licensee of the Black Horse pub.

Bob Carey in 1959 age 20.

Botley's Co-op staff Maureen Shorter (of Boars Hill, later Clarke) and Jackie Smith at the time of its closure in the 1980s. Other staff over the years had, amongst others, included Stella Van Gucci (née Faulkner), Ken Murray, Mr Matthews, Rose Parker, Doris Cripps, Margaret Stone and Margaret Ballard. (Oxford Mail & Times)

Medical Care

The Doctors

The doctors surgery at the West Way end of Elms Road which was demolished in the mid 1990s. Previously, Dr Henry Dempsey and Dr Aubrey Jackson had treated patients at 78 Westminster Way (then Southern By Pass).

Dr Dempsey

The present day surgery at the other end of the same road which was opened in 1992 under the direction of the senior partner, Dr John Slater.

Vale House, West Way

As long ago as 1967, Miss Irene Field of 89 West Way had offered 1.03 acres of adjoining land for elderly persons' accommodation. However, it wasn't until 1986 that work initially started on this site to build council flats and bungalows to provide accommodation for over 60 people and cope with the increased demand from the elderly for the council bungalows in nearby Seacourt Road. Field House was named after the Field family who had first acquired the West Way land in 1902 before having a house built there in about 1930.

From the demolition of 89 and 89a West Way, Vale House, a home for those suffering from Alzheimers disease, was completed in early 1990. On 20 November 1990, the Princess of Wales (then Her Royal Highness), officially opened the premises. On 8 February 1999, famous novelist and philosopher, Dame Iris Murdoch, died at Vale House, aged 79, which by then was a hospice.

Hubert Field with his son Basil and Basil's wife Amy in 1950. Basil's sister Irene also lived in West Way for many years.

89/89a West Way in the 1960s.

Visit of Diana Princess of Wales, outside Field House, West Way, Botley.

Nursing Association

In 1938 parish councillors William Hart, Miss Toynbee and Walter Parker met with the WI to discuss the formation of a Nursing Association which started on 1st April of that year.

Walter and Alice Parker of Arcadia, North Hinksey Lane.

Walter's wife Alice helped out with the baby clinics, held in the WI Hall on North Hinksey Lane for many years. After Elms Court was built in 1968, the clinics were held there. District Nurses Miss I Hale and Miss D Hill, both of 18 Raleigh Park Road, moved to the area in the 1950s and helped their patients for many years.

Cumnor Rise Hospital

Cumnor Rise Hospital was first opened off of Cumnor Rise Road in about 1907 as a home for 'Feeble Minded Girls.' After Miss Tarrant (matron) and Mrs Howarth (lady supt.) came Miss Haigh, who was in charge during the inter-war years. Sadly, many of the residents were simply, lively well-to-do young ladies, who had disgraced their parents. In the pre-NHS days the home tried to be as self-supporting as possible, keeping chickens and having a vegetable garden. Even in the age of the welfare state, the residents would try and do work where possible. Subsequent matrons included Miss Evans, Miss E Hadwen, Mrs Boyd, Miss Bohn from Hungary, Mrs Reid, Wilhelm Statter and Shirley Freestone.

The exterior buildings.

The dining room decorated for Christmas in the 1940s.

Resident Emma 'Maria' Parsons and Miss Bohn.   Edith Jefferies.

When Maria Parsons died in 1983, aged 86, Rowena Bunney, who had worked at the hospital since the 1950s, arranged for her ashes to be buried in Botley cemetery with Maria's best friend and fellow resident Edith Jefferies, who had died in 1978. Another resident, Myrtle Holt, married her sweetheart Bill at St Peter & St Paul's Church in the 1980s.

Matron Miss Haigh with members of the committee.

Church Life

North Hinksey Church

Stephen 'Algernon' Bloxham left £250 in his will for a new altar window in North Hinksey Church following his death aged 63 in 1930. At the time he was living in Kensington, Middlesex although he was born, according to his birth certificate, at "North Hinksey House, Folley Bridge, North Hinksey." His maternal grandfather was Thomas Hall, a London-born boat builder who lived and worked near Folly Bridge in Oxford, which was then in the parish of North Hinksey. His father (also Stephen) was a bank manager and his paternal grandfather was a billiard table keeper at no 113 ½ / 114 St Aldates, which in recent years has housed Barclays Bank and Bradford and Bingley. Stephen Algernon Bloxham's ashes were buried in a grave of the Hall family just outside North Hinksey Church, underneath a tree. Buried in the chancel is Thomas Willis, father of renowned physician Dr Thomas Willis. Dr Willis, amongst many other achievements in the 17th century, detected sugar as an indicator of diabetes.

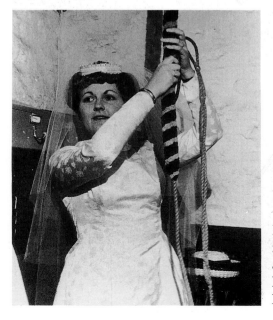

Bellringer Jean Orton on the day of her wedding to Bob Rivers in 1964 at North Hinksey Church. The couple were later involved, with others, in fundraising around £2,000 for the church bells which had fallen into disrepair. (Photograph by Roger Lambert)

North Hinksey and Botley's vicar, Rev John Larter in 1972 with the Bishop of Dorchester, the Right Rev Peter Walker behind the 2 new bells and 4 re-cast ones. The work was carried out by Whites of Appleton. (Oxford Mail & Times)

The 2 vicars who succeeded John Larter are shown below at the christening of then curate Chris Brice's son Peter, in August 1984. Left to right: John Strain, Ann Day (hidden), Rev Peter Rye, (vicar 1984 until his death in 1994, aged 64) Chris Brice, Kate Brice holding son Peter, Canon John Crisp, Judith Burnie. John Crisp, (vicar 1978-1984), from his love of church holidays, was once described as an 'ecclesiastical Billy Butlin.' He died in 1989 aged 70.

St Peter & St Paul's church

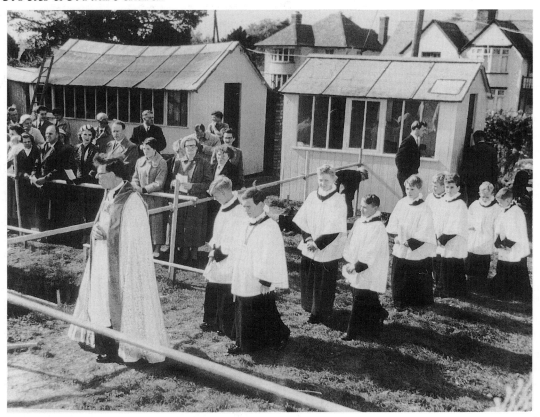

A church procession led by Rev James Stratton for the laying of the foundation stone of St Peter & St Paul's in September 1957. (Oxford Mail & Times)

A visit in May 1999 by former MP for Tatton, Neil Hamilton with his wife Christine, standing either side of Rev Rosie Bates. They were attending a service held at SS Peter & Paul's Church to commemorate the 20th anniversary of the ordination of the Rev David Johnson, a mutual friend of Rosie and the Hamiltons.

Oxford Diocesan Church House

In 1959 the Oxford Diocesan Church House moved its headquarters to the North Hinksey vicarage with the Rev Stratton living in Hurst Rise Road with his second wife (the widowed Mrs Ringrose). The new vicarage was subsequently built next to St Peter and St Paul in Botley.

The picture on the right, taken in September 1991, shows a cross being added to an almost completed extension. The extra space was for a small conference hall and more office accommodation, enabling the Schools Department to move into the building. Left to right: David Rathbone (architect), Stephen Pound (site manager), John Prodger (Chairman of the Diocesan Board of Finance), Tinm Oseman (contracts manager). (Frank Blackwell)

In March 1999, the Archbishop of Canterbury, Dr George Carey and his wife Eileen, made an official 4 day visit to the Oxfordshire diocese which covers Berks, Bucks and Oxfordshire. They are shown here with the Bishop of Oxford, the Right Rev Richard Harries and staff and friends at the Diocesan Church House. (Frank Blackwell)

Our Lady of the Rosary

The Roman Catholic church at the bottom of Yarnells Hill was opened on 24 January 1954. A service of dedication was held later in the year by Archbishop King of Portsmouth and the preacher was Father Thomas of Blackfriars, who was a member of a Cumnor family. A year later the entrance porch was added with an organ installed in 1957 when the Lady Chapel Baptistry and tower were built.

Rev John Crozier christening Donna Chatting in 1965. Left to right: Jim Chatting, John Crozier, Donna held by her mother Joan, Charlie Pitson, Annalisa Dee.

Rev John Crozier blessing the Rosary Room which was being officially opened by Dr H A Dempsey (in front of the car) in 1967. The cedar-wood building was designed by a local parishioner.

A group of houses were built in 1985 in a new road off of Yarnells Hill that was named Crozier Close as a tribute to the nearby church's 1st priest. Scots-born Crozier (later a Canon) (1917-1993) was responsible for seeing the completion of Our Lady of the Rosary Church in North Hinksey (started by his predecessor, Father Hickey) as well as being a driving force in the building of churches in Wootton (St Pius X), Boars Hill (St Thomas More), South Oxford (Holy Rood) and Kennington (Good Shepherd). It wasn't long before he had a timber-built bungalow built next to the North Hinksey church which he had designed himself.

Rev Peter Codd, the Roman Catholic Priest, at the wedding of Vanessa Miller to Colm Toner on 16 August 1997.

Rev Hamper's holiday to Keswick in the mid 1950s. Back row, left to right: – Woodward, Don Savins, David Errington, Brian 'John' Errington, Bob Rivers, Peter Junor, Alan Trafford, – Delamare, Stan Lanchbury, John Skinner. 2nd row: George Deacon, –, Gill (Savins), Mavis Derrick, Briony Delafield, Susan Baxter, Ann Trinder, – Wren, Wendy Haines, Gill Broome, Paul Innes. 3rd row: Zorah Ashraf, Rita Savins, –, –, Rev Richard Hamper, Grace Roberts, –, Dorothy Hayward, Pauline Adams. Front row: –, –, Cliff Cose, –, Terry Philips, –, Derek Rivers, Robert Woodforde.

John Crisp's church holiday to North Wales in 1983. Eunice Townsend (née Tilby) is the 4th from the left in the middle row. The 2 ladies on chairs are Nancy Robinson's mother Dorothy Hicks (left) and Elsie Lane of Yarnells Hill (right), a retired school teacher who died in 1999. Matthew Ford is sat between them in front of Francis Barker.

Hedley Feast, Botley's Baptist minister since 1997. Born at the Radcliffe Infirmary, Hedley grew up in Gaisford Road, Cowley where he attended the John Bunyan Baptist Church nearby. Wanting to be a minister since his teens, Hedley first spent a few years at Cowley works doing admin work while preparing for his vocation. Through his ministry work, he has known other Botley ministers from John Matthews through to his predecessor David Rowland. A strong supporter of local radio, he has long been involved with BBC Radio Oxford/Thames Valley and has broadcast the station's Sunday morning religious programme for the past few years.

St Andrew's Church

St Andrew's Church and hall in Dean Court was built in 1961 to meet the need of the growing population there. Previously, from February 1956 until December 1961, church services had been held at Dean Court's Community Centre. A history of the church was written by Michael G Harris, he had played a large part in the planning and construction of the building.

Sport and Societies

Botley United Football Club in 1953. Top row, left to right: Tony Carey, Ken Brentnall, Ray Ball, Mike Robinson, Basil Wheeler. Bottom row: Bill Wheeler, George Wheeler (known as 'Scaffy'), Eddie Wheeler, Ronnie Havard, Ted Tidbury, Horace Evans (captain).

Clive Walker, who lived at Chestnut Road, became a professional footballer, achieving success as a left winger for Chelsea, followed by other teams, QPR, Sunderland, Fulham and Brighton. For the 1997/98 season Clive was assistant manager for Brentford. His nephew, Keith Holmes, was also a professional footballer, at one time playing for Oxford United.

Botley School football team c1967. Back row, left to right: Robert Scrivens, Richard Gordon, Jeremy Bowles, Chris Dennis, Vaughan Jagger. Front row: Martyn Coombs, Peter French, Stephen Powell?, Clive Walker, Alan Rowe and Paul Donohoe.

Botley Boys Football Club
Botley Boys Football Club was revived in 1992 after a lapse of 26 years. Its first President was Steve McLaren, then coach to Oxford United, now assistant manager at Manchester United. After only six weeks the club won its first trophy — at the Launton Boys Six-a-Side Tournament.

Under 8s Six-a-Side winners in 1992. Standing, left to right: Marcus Ashcroft Jones, Jonathan Buckingham, Nickey Massey, William Jones. Sitting: Ryan Curtin, Louis Masters, Andrew Morton.

The teams used the pitch and facilities of Botley Men's Football Club on Arnolds Way and also the sports field of Botley School.

Under 10s team 1994. Standing, left to right: Robin Masters (joint manager), Matthew Robbins, Tom Barton, Ryan Curtin, Jamie Hornblow, Tommy O'Driscoll, Kevin Burch, Nicky Massey and David Curtin (joint manager). Sitting: Steven Jordan, Tom Sheppard, Jordan Reid, Kevin Fry, Louis Masters, Andrew Morton, Carl Palin, and Luke Westell.

For two years there were also girls' teams but the enthusiasm did not last, although young girls still play in younger mixed teams. The club began negotiations with Cumnor Parish Council for use of the recreation field that was an integral part of the Fogwell development. The first fixtures there were played in the 1996/7 season. The Parish Council, with support from the club and grants from the National Lottery Fund and the Sports Council, built a pavilion at the ground, as they were required to do by their ground lease from the University. The pavilion was opened on 18 February 1998 by Malcolm Shotton, manager of Oxford United, and Malcom Crosby, assistant manager of West Bromwich Albion. The club has been very successful, winning local trophies, while several youngsters have had trials with professional teams.

'Pavilioned in splendour ...'

Scouts

Both the 4th and 15th Oxford Scouts have been based in Botley using the scout hut in Arnolds Way and the Baptist Church Hall respectively. The 4th Oxford Scouts (originally formed in 1908) moved from Beef Lane, St Ebbes to their new premises in the early 1970s. It was officially opened in 1974. Some of those involved in the scouts in Botley over the years have included Jim Whale (scout leader), Stan Litten (group chairman), Ted and Ann Lainchbury, Terry Saxton, John Weston (group scout leader) John Kemp (chairman), Connie Bodey (cub scout leader), Dave Level (chairman), Mary Smith and Anne Greening.

A group of the 4th Oxford Scouts in 1975 with scout leader Jim Whale.

1 Tim Ashwell, 2 —, 3 Tim Weston, 4 —, 5 Mark Baxter, 6 —, 7 —, 8 David? Peedell, 9 Richard Morton, 10 Stephen Honour, 11 David Butler, 12 Clive Scrivens, 13 Paul Litten, 14 —, 15 Geoff —, 16 Paul Scothorn, 17 Stuart Talbot (from South Hinksey), 18 Brian Morgan, 19 Marcus Kemp.

Brownies & Guides

Margaret Ballard (right) got involved in the Brownies in 1969 assisting Dorothy Stepney with the 1st Botley Brownies where they would meet in the 'tin hut' church hall. As the demand increased so the 2nd Botley Brownies was established in 1972 with Angela Bye as 'Brown Owl.' In the 1970s they met in the church hall, next to SS Peter & Paul's church until moving to the scout hut on Lime Road.

1st and 2nd Botley Brownies in the late 1980s. The guiders in the front row are, left to right: Lucy Howes (née Pheysey-Jones), Dorothy Stepney, Alison Griffin, Margaret Ballard, Doreen Buckingham.

After being a Brownie from the age of 7–10, many would then join the guides. Shown here are some of the 1st Botley Guides in December 1989. In the centre is guider Pauline Lloyd (née Cox), with guider Diana Backhouse on her immediate left. Mrs Gledhill (Gem) is 2nd from left. Previous guiders included Mrs Butler and Pamela Thomas.

The Parish Council

The first entry in an early North Hinksey Parish Council minute book was for a meeting on 19th April, 1934 at 8pm in North Hinksey School. Those present were John Curtis, Frank Curtis, Ernest Carey, Isaac Bawden and Hector Wigg (chair). Mr J Smith of North Lodge, Old Botley was appointed clerk being paid £10/year. Winifred Toynbee and Ellis Wren were at the next meeting held in John Curtis' office.

Some of the North Hinksey parish councillors in 1958. Left to right: C Egan (clerk), Sam Snelson, Anthony Jordan, Stan Brogden. Stan Brogden was a member of the parish council 1949–1979, and was chairman in 1954/5 and 1961-1979. Upn his retirement he was presented with a bottle of whisky and a book token. (Oxford Mail & Times)

Outside Seacourt Hall on voting day for the European elections on 6 June 1999, with Anthony Gresswell (co-owner of Hinksey Heights Golf Course) and Ann Dykes.

Some of the North Hinksey parish councillors, just before attending a meeting in July 1999. Left to right: Alexandra Brown, Austin Griffiths, Sandra Dwek, Ted Beaver, John Kemp, Eric Batts, Barry Ford, Ans Laver, Julia Bishop (clerk), Pam Johnston.

Briony Newport (née Delafield), who was elected chair of North Hinksey Parish Council in 1999 grew up in Botley. When her mother 'Dela' Delafield was expecting her, she spoke to the Charlton family then on the corner of West Way and the Southern By Pass. There was a wildflower growing all over the garden wall and on being told it was called 'Bryony' (a flower that rambles all over hedges) she decided that if she gave birth to a daughter, she would call her by that name , although spelling it with an 'i' instead of a 'y.'

Briony was born in 1941 at 62 Montagu Road, delivered by her mother just before the midwife from Finmore Road arrived. The Montagu Road house was rented from decorator Mr Baker, as Briony's father, engineer/toolmaker Charles, a man of principle, at that time disapproved of house ownership. After marrying, Briony lived in West Oxford although still maintained very strong links with the Botley community. The family moved to Stanley Close in 1981. Serving the community was always in Briony's blood as her grandmother had been a county councillor and city mayor in Hartlepool. Briony, herself became a district councillor for the Vale in 1991 (re-elected in 1995 and in 1999 when she was made vice-chair), a North Hinksey School governor that same year and a parish councillor in 1995.

Friends of North Hinksey in 1967. Miss Best (centre) is looking at a model of North Hinksey with her mother (right) as it might have looked in the 1840s. (Oxford Mail & Times)

An Over 60s Miss World contest held at Elms Court in 1970. Emmie Prytherch is in the centre in between 2nd place Miss Spain (Dorothy Cooper) and judge Harry Keene. Winifred Jaques came 1st as Miss Japan and Daisy Harris (far right) was 3rd as Miss Ireland. (Oxford Mail & Times)

Women's Institute

Botley WI came 1st in a competition held at Wytham Abbey in June 1937 in which local WIs had to dress up as a family group. Botley's Victorian family beat off competiton from Wytham (2nd as a sheikh and his wives) and Cumnor (a Japanese family). Left to right: Alice Parker, –, Miss Thackeray, Bill 'Professor' Austin, Rene Launchbury, Nellie Read.

More members of Botley WI dressed up in about 1930. Those identified include, back row: Mrs Harris (large hat right of banner), Pearce Enoch (3rd from right). 2nd row: Lily Hawtin (3rd from left with daughter Barbara 2nd from left front row), Nan Enoch (large hat below right of Mrs Harris), Mrs Floyd (left of spear). Seated row: Mrs Church and Elsie Herbert (1st and 2nd from left), Mrs Hull (bow tie) left of Miss Thackeray (crucifix), Mrs Parker (4th from right).

Remembering the Wars

First World War (1914–1918)

The North Hinksey Church war memorial lists the following 'Ferry Hinksey/Botley' soldiers who were killed in World War I:

Barson, Thomas	Daniels, James	Parsons, Alfred
Barson, William	Finch, Walter	Pimm, Daniel
Bradfield, Walter	Jenkins, Frank	Weaver, William
Cooper, Thomas	Lewington, William	White, William,

130119 Pioneer, William G Barson, Royal Engineers, who died 29 October1916 age 17, has a headstone in North Hinksey churchyard. Private Thomas Frederick Barson 241963 (ex 5863) 2nd/5th Bn Suffolk Regiment died 5 May 1917 age 30. He lived at 4 Old Botley.

Second World War (1939-1945)

In 1939, with the outbreak of war, many children were evacuated from Poplar in London to Botley and North Hinksey. 13 year old Dan Duhig (later a Bevan boy) was initially sent to Mr and Mrs Hedges at College Farm, North Hinksey village whilst his 6 year old sister Mary was at the neighbouring Manor Farm with the Tilby family and later lived with the Harpers by the cemetery. There was a brother and sister from another London family who were billeted to College Farm and the Fishes respectively, but soon returned to London where they were tragically killed in the Blitz. Dan was moved to the Ayres family at Victoria Cottage (a house now demolished opposite where the Black Horse was) and later the Harrises at 30 Poplar Road before moving with his mother and the family to Homelea in Old Botley. The Duhigs remained in Botley becoming an important and well known part of the community.

The Duhig children in the 1930s. Top to bottom: James, Patrick, Dan, Mary and Bernie.

Jack Day in his uniform on leave from the Royal Air Force during the Second World War. He joined up in 1938 and spent time away in Scotland and the Far East returning in 1946 to settle down to married life with his wife Clementine. When they lived in a caravan site in garden of 'The Fishes' some of the prisoners of war would cut wood for them when they were nearby clearing and tidying rivers.

Plane Crash in Yarnells Road

On 12 June 1940, pilot Charles Alan Washer, age 29 of Almondsbury, near Thornbury, Gloucestershire, was tragically killed when his plane crashed at the top of Yarnells Road (on the south east side). Heroically, Washer managed to avoid all houses and people apart from slightly clipping a nearby chimney roof. He was testing a civilian plane, a Bristol Beaufort prototype serial no. L4443. (He had been with the aeroplane manufacturers, Bristol, since about 1935). It is believed that there were other members of the crew with two bailing out at Port Meadow when the engine caught fire and the co-pilot also escaping despite being badly burnt. The gardener at nearby Timbers, Mr Hall, who was out in the garden, promptly lay down on the ground as the plane approached. Joyce Nickolls and her niece Peggy immediately went along to investigate and were met with this tragic scene. Many others, particularly children who had just come out of school, went along to see what had happened, some later retrieving bits of metal debris from the wreckage. Rumours wrongly spread, perhaps for security reasons by policeman Sharky Adams, that it was a Canadian crew that had crashed. In another crash towards the end of the war, a pilot survived when his glider landed near the Hurst where Stanville Road now is.

Just slightly further south along the bypass, there were many tanks parked between the turn for North Hinksey and South Hinksey. Quite a few people learnt to drive on the bypass which was usually a quiet road. They would be greatly disturbed by the approach of a large tank in their vicinity.

Prisoner of War Camp

In 1942, a prisoner of war camp was opened at the top of Harcourt Hill. One of these prisoners was Yugoslav, Mr Judt who ran the shop Lanka.

Prisoners of war, Herman and Arno, who worked for farmer Bill Grant.

John Briggs, as a child, visited the camp and ate there, as a result of a cook sergeant being billeted at his parents' house in Raleigh Park Road. Children would go up to the camp observing the prisoners sometimes taking them food. They appeared friendly and happy, sometimes playing football bare-footed. They lived in one-storey barracks in grounds enclosed by a barbed-wire fence. The Italians, after changing sides during the war, had their restrictions on movement lifted. Once released, quite a few of the prisoners would help the local farmers, as many of Britain's men were still away.

The prisoners were quite industrious producing items such as ashtrays (pottery and copper), shoes, bone carvings and jewellery boxes. There are some reports that suggest that officers of the German Navy were also held at Harcourt Hill.

After the prisoners were repatriated in 1947, interest arose in using the property for housing. In 1948 however, the Labour Officer of the Agricultural Executive Committee wrote to the parish council stating that the camp was being used as a hostel for civilian workers in agriculture and that there was not likely to be vacant accommodation for housing any other community. The next year the Pressed Steel Company acquired the camp to house some of its workers. Pictured on the right are food tins found near the site of the Prisoner of War camp in the early 1970s.

A portrait of 15 year old apprentice electrician Jim Hainge who cycled up Harcourt Hill to the camp from his home on the Cutteslowe estate. He was working there for Lindars Electrical Contractors (Oxford) Ltd with a colleague George Robinson. The drawing dated 22 November 1942, was sketched (from a photo of Jim in his army cadet uniform) by Italian prisoner of war Pigni Ubaldo of 'Fagnano Olona' from the province of Varese near Milan.

In the early 1980s, Jim Hainge and his family moved to a house he built on Harcourt Hill.

ARP (Air Raid Precaution)

Members of the local ARP who would meet in places like the Baptist church (when it was in West Way) and in Stanley Close. The two ladies on the right are Nancy Enoch and her sister Cilla Brett. Barbara Hawtin is 3rd from the right. Mr Soden is 5th from left. Mrs King was an ambulance driver for them and Mr Wissett was in charge. One of the sheds at the Fishes was used as a workshop for making packing cases.

A 1945 street party in Montagu Road (looking towards the Finmore/Crabtree Road junction) celebrating the end of hostilities. The 1st 4 ladies on the left side (nearest to furthest away): Mrs Boreham, Frances Shirley, Rene Norman, Jesse Freebury (Jean Walker is the 3rd child along). On the right, nearest to the front is Mrs Trafford and furthest is Mrs Telling. Philip Jones is at the far end of the table.

A VJ (Victory in Japan) Party at 'The Fishes.' On the left side nearest is Pat Loxton followed by Hazel Tilby. Mary Ovenell is the 5th face along. On the right side at the front is May Kerton with her daughter Linda. May's husband, Stan, was once secretary of the Master Butcher's Association, a North Hinksey parish councillor and was involved in starting the Botley and North Hinksey Social Club. He died in 1999 aged 90.

The Falklands War

Ian Lainchbury joined the Army when aged 16½ after leaving Matthew Arnold School. He was a gunner in the Falklands war and returned to Britain on 11 July 1982 arriving at Southampton on the Canberra. A hero's welcome awaited him at Sycamore Road — the family home. The road was adorned with bunting and flags and a large banner saying 'Welcome Home Ian.' Even the local vicar, John Crisp, brought round some beer for the celebration.

Ian Lainchbury arriving back in the country from the Falkland Islands.

Ian's parents, Ted and Ann Lainchbury (below), first moved to Botley in 1960. Ted was a toolsetter at the Radiators in Cowley working alongside toolmaker George Lane of Stanley Close. Over the years, Ted and Ann have been involved in many aspects of Botley and North Hinksey life such as the cubs and scouts, the church and the Fishes' fêtes. Secretarial work for the local vicar John Crisp resulted in Ann working at Diocesan Church House from 1979 to 1996. Ted was on the PCC (Parochial Church Council) and deanery synod as well as being a sidesman at St Peter & St Paul's. For over 30 years he has helped out at Elms Road Nursery, whether it be repairing toys or doing some gardening.

The 50th Anniversary of V.E. Day in 1995 was celebrated in Botley and North Hinksey by events ranging from a memorial service in the Commonwealth Grave section of Botley Cemetery to a garden fête, children's sports, outdoor theatre and ending with the lighting of a beacon.

Local clergy, including Douglas Durand and David Rowland, lead the memorial service.

Children's sports afternoon.

Young people relaxing at the skateboard park. The guitar shaped bowl had been officially opened in 1991 following fund-raising by the Botley SK8s (whose chairman was Angela 'Ag' Mackeith) and support from the parish council.

Sandra Dwek, Julia Bishop and Pamela Johnston, organisers of many of the day's events.

Lighting the beacon to end a chilly but rewarding summer's day.

People

The Rivers family

Frederick and Iris Rivers moved from West Oxford to Arthray Road (then 13 Elms Rise estate) in the latter half of the 1930s. It was here in Botley that they brought up their children Mick, Bob, Derek, Jean and Paul and soon established themselves as one of the most well known families in the community. Right: Frederick and Iris in the 1930s.

Left: The Rivers children, left to right: Jean, Mick, Derek, cousin Jennifer Major, Bob. Above: Paul Rivers.

Mick and Bob Rivers sat on the street corner just outside the Seacourt Bridge Inn, a very popular meeting place for the youths of the 1950s.

The Bishop family

The Bishop family moved from Woodstock to Botley during the First World War, initially living in one of the cottages on the site of the Seacourt Bridge Inn where Mrs Bishop's parents, the Pearces, lived. They then moved to North Hinksey village.

The wedding of Florence Edith Bishop to Albert Edward Allsworth (of South Hinksey) on 1 December 1928 on the Green in North Hinksey village. Standing, left to right: Alice Bishop, groom & bride, bestman Bert Bishop, Florence Allsworth (later Earl). Seated: Ellen Bishop (later Badnell), Kathleen Bishop, Gertrude Bishop.

A photo of the Bishop family taken in the WI Hall in 1949 to celebrate the golden wedding anniversary of Walter and Edith Bishop. Included in the photo are their 10 children. Back row, left to right: Ern 'Bonnie' Bishop, Kathleen Wigger, Fred Bishop, Gertrude Griffin, Harry Bishop, Ellen Badnell. Front row: Walt Bishop junior, Bert Bishop, Walter & Edith, Florence Allsworth, Alice 'Maud' Harvey. Walter senior died in 1955 aged 79 and Edith died in 1967 aged 87.

Many members of the Bishop family have been milkmen (Walt junior's son, Vic Bishop, retired from his round in Sutton Courtenay in 1999). Around the Botley area Harry Bishop (who died in 1988 aged 75) was a merry character as he delivered his milk by horse and cart. John Edgington recalled how the children would help push his cart up Crabtree Road during the snowy weather. Harry also taught John how to fish for pike in the village stream.

Harry Bishop's milk float outside what was number 8 Ferry Hinksey when the Bishops moved into the cottage just after the First World War. (Oxford Mail & Times)

John Errington
In September 1959, police-man John Errington of North Hinksey Lane, was knocked off his motorcycle by a car in Bicester whilst on a training drive. As an acknowledgement to his bravery, the John Errington Fund was soon established to promote Oxford police efficiency and make awards to policemen. He remained in a wheelchair until his death in the early 1980s aged 42.

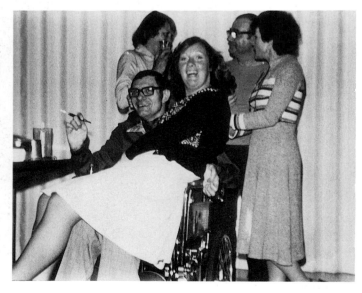

The Parkins/Winchester/Holmes family

In 1935, John and Emily Parkins, bought a new house on the Southern By Pass (later Westminster Way), having previously lived in Sadler Street (St Ebbe's) and Bridge Street (Osney). The land on which the houses were built was previously partly owned by Stephen Howse. Prior to 1921, the land was owned by the Earl of Abingdon. The house, 'Audreyvilla,' has remained in the same family ever since. Their daughter, Edith, who died aged 53 of cancer, had one daughter, Audrey Winchester, who moved into the house in 1957 after her marriage to Clive Holmes. Emily Parkins (née Slatter) was a relation of St John Ambulance man Harold Slatter, who bought a house in Beech Road when they were first built in the 1950s. John Parkins was head maintenance man at Worcester College.

Audrey, as a young child with her father, William Winchester (left) and grandfather John Parkins (right).

Adults with Audrey, left to right: grandparents John and Emily Parkins, mother Edith.

Clive Holmes in the front garden with daughter Sandra.

Henry Francies (1904-1994)

Henry Francies came from his native Essex to Botley in 1976 to be nearer family and grandchildren in his retirement. A modest and generous gentleman with a great sense of humour who delighted in meeting people, he was able to devote himself to his life-long interest in painting and drawing. For over 17 years, his skill and enthusiasm was passed on to the many members of his adult art classes at Matthew Arnold School and other groups in the area. His work has been shown at the Pastel Society in London and other national exhibitions.

He continued to teach until his 90th birthday when sadly he died just before a party which had been arranged by his students to present him with a book of their works as a token of their appreciation. Henry particularly enjoyed drawing buildings, an example of which may be seen in his line drawing of St Lawrence Church (right) on the cover of the parish church magazine.

In the summer months, he encouraged his students to draw outside at the local farms and churches in North Hinksey, Binsey and Cumnor. Each year, examples of their work was on show at an exhibition in the Baptist Church Hall. The work of this much loved local artist still continues to give pleasure in numerous houses in Britain and abroad.

Henry Francies demonstrating his skills.

Henry's grandson, Guy Browning, who came to Botley as a child in 1970, has achieved quite a lot of success in various fields. In the latter half of the 1980s, he appeared on the re-vamped TV talent show 'New Faces' as part of a comedy duo called 'Dros Bros.' Stern critic and tabloid journalist Nina Myskow was greatly entertained by them. In recent years, Guy has written witty articles for 'The Guardian' newspaper. Here, he is seen in 1989 in Botley Shopping Centre, standing by an advert for which he was responsible for the slogan.

The Backhouse Family

The Backhouse family came to Laburnum Road in 1960 from Chester Street, off the Iffley Road. George and Mary, who had met working at Blackwells, soon got involved in running the over 60s club. Mary was one of the founder members of the Botley Towns-women's Guild and has also been greatly involved in the Mothers' Union. George, who died in 1993, sang for the operatic societies in Abingdon and Kennington. George had a love of entertaining. At one time he had a group of locals in his living room arranging a version of 'Widdecombe Fair' that was to be performed for a church entertainment evening. It was daughter Geraldine Backhouse (later Blake) who encouraged her parents to go to church when she was being confirmed. Their other daughter, Diana, was a guider for many years.

Mary and George Backhouse (seated) with daughters behind them: Diana (left), Geraldine (right).

Dorothy Squires

Widow Dorothy Squires (shown here in 1984), grew up in Shellingford and moved to Elms Road from Oxford's Leckford Road in the late 1960s. A popular narrator, she has often delighted others with her poems and prose using her interest in the observation of life around her. She celebrated her 98th birthday in 1999 with a trip to Paris organised by vicar Rev Rosie Bates.

Stephen Edward Howse

Who knows what Botley would have been like if the Howse family had never come here? Elms Parade is still as relevant today as it was in 1937 and still owned by the Howse family. It is fitting that when he died in 1941, Stephen Howse was buried in Botley cemetery.

At one time farming about 1,000 acres in the Botley/North Hinksey area (including Elms Farm, Seacourt Farm and Hutchcomb Farm), the Howse name has been known in Botley since their arrival in 1916. The farming era finished in 1963 when eldest son Eddie Howse moved to Milestone Farm in Banbury to breed racehorses.

Botley Library

Leonard Harwood being served by librarian, Ann Thomas at Botley Library. Formerly the Library was in Elms Farm House.

PRIVATE RESIDENTS

Allsworth Noah, Botley Pound
Ashfield Frederick, 28 Poplar Road
Avery George, 19 Poplar Road
Ayres Henry
Ayres Thomas
Barson Joseph
Barson Matthew John
Barson Mrs M
Barson Thomas
Bateman William Charles
Beal George
Bennett George
Bennett Lionel, Elm Croft, Cumnor Hill
Bennett William Henry
Blackwell George Henry Bertie, The Rosary, Botley Pound
Bowler George, 7 Poplar Road
Bradfield Frederick James, 8 Poplar Road
Brown William Herbert, Lulworth
Bryant James
Burden Frederick, Crookham House
Carter Mrs, 5 Poplar Road
Chennell Wm, Inglenook, Botley Pound
Charlton Alfred John, Harmsworth
Cheshire Thomas, Botley Pnd
Church William
Coates William Charles
Cooper James, 17 Poplar Road
Cooper John Wm, Bexhill, Botley Pound
Cox Frederick, 16 Poplar Road
Curtis Ernest, Kenilworth
Curtis Frank Robert, Briardene
Curtis John T, Broad Clyst Hse
Curtis Mrs, North Lodge
Curtis William, Seacourt Villa
Dale Rev J G MA [Vicar]
Enoch James, 7 Elms Road
Enoch William J, 1 Poplar Road
Field Edward John, Ferndell
Finch Mrs, 11 Poplar Road
Fletcher George, Botley Pound
Floyd Mrs
Grove Thomas W, 6 Elms Road
Hale Owen
Harris Alfred, 30 Poplar Road

Harris Frank, 4 Poplar Road
Hastings William, 15 Poplar Rd
Hawtin George, 12 Poplar Road
Hayman Charles
Hayter James Lawrence, Cumnor Hill
Hedderly Mrs, Stud Farm
Hedges James, Botley Pound
Hemmings William, Elms Lodge
Hill George, Mayfield, Botley Pound
Hollis Mrs, 3 Poplar Road
Howe Arthur Swithin, Oak Dene, Botley Pound
Hudson Henry
Jarvis Frederick E, 6 Poplar Rd
King George
King Harold, 22 Poplar Road
Kitchen Mrs
Launchbury James, 2 Poplar Rd
Lewington Geo, Singletree, Botley Pound
Limbrick Frederick, 21 Poplar Rd
Lovegrove Wilfrid, Halcombe Villa
Mullington Albt Emmanuel, Botley Pound
Morbey Mrs, 18 Poplar Road
Moss Frederick William Neale Alfred L, 13 Poplar Rd
Ovenell Henry, Eynsham Road
Pearce Albert V, 9 Poplar Rd
Pearce Percival , 23 Poplar Rd
Pickett Mrs
Pimm John, 10 Poplar Road
Pratley Mrs, Ferndale
Price Joseph, Botley Pound
Qurtish Henry Thomas
Raleigh Sir Walter knt, MA, The Hangings
Read Alfred
Read Joseph Barnes, Victoria Cottage
Ridge Charles, Botley Pound
Ridge James
Roberts Mrs, Belvedere
Robinette John Walter, Tramore
Saunders James, 8 Elms Road
Smith R W, North Lodge
Stanmore Alfred, Hopewell
Stayte John, 1 Elms Road
Sturch William G, 24 Poplar Rd

Thomas Percy, 5 Elms Road
Tilby William F, The Priory
Trinder Arthur, Ivyhurst
Turner Thomas Arnatt, Tanglewood, Botley Pound
Venables John, Willowdene
Warburton Mrs S, The Limes, Botley Pound
Watson Ernest John, Egremont, Botley Pound
Webb Mrs, 18 Poplar Road
Webb Noah, 14 Poplar Road
Wigg Charles Hector, Hillside
Woodbridge Fred, 20 Poplar Rd

COMMERCIAL

Botley Post Office (William Hemmings, sub-postmaster)
Bull William Alfred, shopkeeper
Burden Frederick, blacksmith, Cumnor Hill
Carey Ernest George, grocer
Curtis John & Sons, engineers & dealers in agricultural implements, Botley works. See advertisement
Curtis Stphn Hy, farmer, Sweatsman's Farm
Daniels Frederick, The George PH
Greening William, farmer, Hinksey Hill
Harris Henry, The Fishes Inn
Hedges Mrs, farmer, Manor Farm
Hedges William, farmer, College Farm
Jefferies Frederick CK, police constable
Oxford University Rifle Club (range)
Hancox Spencer, The Black Horse PH
Howse S, farmer, Elms Farm
Jefferies Frederick CK, police constable
Phillips Alfd Hy, The Carpenters Arms PH
Robinson John, blacksmith
Surman William, baker
Turner Albt Vincent, farmer, Seacourt Farm
White William, supt of City of Oxford Cemetery, Botley

Rev James Stratton with a group of local people, probably in the 1940s/50s. Back row: Mrs Woodbridge, Mrs Harper, Mrs Greenwood (1st three along, left to right), Mrs Sherlock (5th from left), Nellie Read (6th from left), Alice Parker, Mrs Hainge, Pearce Enoch (4th, 3rd, 2nd from right). Middle Rows, standing: Mrs George? (wearing dark hat, immediately in front of lady left of Nellie Read), Mrs Sims (in front of Mrs Parker), Mrs Floyd (partly hidden and in between Mrs Hainge and Mrs Enoch), Mrs Richards (3rd from right), Mrs Betty Woodbridge (2nd from right). Seated: Mr and Mrs Ayres (behind and either side of Rev Stratton), the first Mrs Stratton (right of Rev Stratton), Mrs Anne Taylor (on the grass next to Mrs Stratton).